SELF- EMPOWERMENT RESET

Business Goddesses

Rev. Dr. Marianne Padjan, Lori McNeil, Amanda M. Renaud, Dr. Andrea Adams-Miller, Tammy Williams, Linda McBee, Nicky Cuesta, Kylee Leota, Denise-Millet-Burkhardt, Bethany Stone, Stephanie Brandolini, Karen Hewitt, Yara Ortiz, Rosemary Ghiz, Ivy Perez, Olga Geidane

Legal Disclaimer

SELF-EMPOWERMENT RESET

BUSINESS GODDESSES Copyright © 2024 MPOWERED WORD PUBLISHING. All rights reserved worldwide. No part of this material may be used, reproduced, distributed, or transmitted in any form and by any means whatsoever, including without limitation photocopying, recording or other electronic or mechanical methods or by any information storage and retrieval system, without the prior written permission from the author, except for brief excerpts in a review. This book is intended to provide general information only. Neither the author nor publisher provides any legal or other professional advice. If you need professional advice, you should seek advice from the appropriate licensed professional. This book does not provide complete information on the subject matter covered. This book is not intended to address specific requirements, either for an individual or an organization. This book is intended to be used only as a general guide, and not as a sole source of information on the subject matter. While the author has undertaken diligent efforts to ensure accuracy, there is no guarantee of accuracy or of no errors, omissions, or typographical errors. Any slights of people or organizations are unintentional. The author and publisher shall have no liability or responsibility to any person or entity and hereby disclaim all liability, including without limitation, liability for consequential damages regarding any claim, loss or damage that may be incurred, or alleged to have been incurred, directly or indirectly, arising out of the information provided in this book.

Connect with MPowered Word Publishing
www.spiritualtouch11@gmail.com

Copyright © 2024 by MPOWERED WORD PUBLISHING

All rights reserved. No part of this publication may be reproduced or transmitted in any form or by any means, electronic, or mechanical, including photocopying, recording, or by any information storage and retrieval system.

~ DEDICATIONS~

I dedicate this book to my mother, myself and all the Women who are working on themselves and doing themselves and doing their best everyday!

~ Rev. Dr. Marianne Padjan

SELF-EMPOWERMENT RESET

~ TABLE OF CONTENTS ~

Contents

Dedication... 3

Foreword......Lori A. McNeil..................... 7

Chapter 1 ..Rev. Dr. Marinanne Padjan.....9

A Goddess Within Was Found....................

Chapter 2..Amanda M. Renaud................ 22

Keep Going Goddess!...........................

Chapter 3..Denise Millett-Burkhardt........36

Business Fostering Kindness, Proactive Listening, Open Communication, and Empowering Women in Embracing the Role of a Goddess in Entrepreneurship

Chapter 4..Dr. Andrea Miller-Adams.........44

The Goddess Within: The Brain and Brawn of Her Success and Power

Chapter 5..Tammy Williams......................64

Discovering Our Inner Business Goddess Through Life Experience

~ TABLE OF CONTENTS ~

Contents

Chapter 6..Linda McBee............................74

Empowering Women in 2025

Chapter 7...Nicky Cuesta........................84

From Corporate Chains to Entrepreneurial Reign

Chapter 8..Yara Ortiz...............................97

From Struggle to CEO, My Self- Empowerment Reset

Chapter 9..Stephanie Brandolini.............105

Hello & Welcome

Chapter 10..Bethany Stone......................120

To Thrive

Chapter 11..Kylee Leota..........................132

The Way of the Goddess in Business

Chapter 12..Rosemary Ghiz....................143

The Power of Unconventional Thinking; Awakening the Goddess Within

~ TABLE OF CONTENTS ~

Contents

Chapter 13..Karen Hewitt....................152

From Chaos to Clarity

Chapter 14..Ivy Perez............................163

A Business Built on Belief: My Story of Self-Trust and Success

Chapter 15..Olga Geidane......................177

The Power of Alignment from Survival to Sovereignty

Acknowledgements................................187

About the Author...................................188

Rev. Dr. Marianne Padjan

~ FOREWORD ~
LORI A. MCNEIL

Women have always been the architects of resilience, the bearers of strength, and the quiet warriors who shape generations. Yet, too often, their voices muted, their stories untold, and their power underestimated. This book is a testament to the undeniable truth that women are pioneers, leaders, and visionaries.

The world today often demands more than it gives, and women continue to rise. They rise in the face of adversity. They rise in moments of uncertainty. They rise when the odds are stacked against them. And they rise not just for themselves, but for those who will follow in their footsteps.

This book is more than a collection of stories, insights, and wisdom, it is a declaration. A declaration that women will no longer wait for permission to step into their greatness. A declaration that the experiences, struggles, and triumphs shared here will serve as a guide for others on the path to empowerment.

SELF-EMPOWERMENT RESET

To the woman reading this now: You are seen. Your journey matters. Whether you are building a business, raising a family, breaking barriers in your field, or simply finding the courage to take your next step, know that you are part of something greater.

This book is here to remind you that your strength is not just in what you do, but in who you are.

Let these words ignite something within you. Let them remind you that you are powerful beyond measure. Above all, let them serve as a rallying call—because when women support each other, we don't just break ceilings; we build new foundations. Welcome to a journey of empowerment, authenticity, and unstoppable courage.

~ Lori McNeil

~ Chapter 1 ~

Rev. Dr. Marianne Padjan

A Goddess Within Was Found

My mother turned around and went home. She told my father that she was pregnant, and my father sent her to a clinic to get an abortion. When she got there she didn't like it, so she turned around and came home. My mother said to my father; "I am having this baby with or without you." Two months later they were married. This is how my life got started, even before I was born. I was not wanted by my father.

When I came out as a female, he wanted me even less. This is how my life had began, and this went on for the next twenty years. My father complaining, and my mother defending me. I spent the next 20, 30 ,40 ,50 and now 60 years healing up. My lack of self-worth was a of lack of self love and my lack of feeling enough!.

This of course is obviously where my lack of self-worth came from, my lack of self-love and my not enough theory was inside of my head. I had my own self sabotaging committee inside of my thought pattern.

SELF-EMPOWERMENT RESET

This had begun my journey to loving myself and learning that I am enough.

This this was just an unfortunate set of circumstances and the way I chose to learn all of my lessons. My father served as a catalyst for most of my issues. This would be the main reason why I blamed him for nearly everything. My father of course did not know any better because he grew up in a family of eleven children, were two of them passed away early on from tuberculosis.

His parents and family barely had enough to even eat. There was hardly ever enough food, let alone any kind of money. Survival was his way of living. That would be the reason why we came to Canada from Croatia. He wanted a better life and a better life for him meant more money.

A few years after we arrived in Canada we discovered that he was actually bipolar, and he needed to go on some pretty heavy medication.

Work was always a priority over anything and if he needed to work overtime he would. If there wasn't enough money for his medication or we didn't have time to go pick it up then that was okay. My mother and I soon discovered that he was anything but okay.

SELF-EMPOWERMENT RESET

We made sure he had medication all the time. We discovered that this medication kept him from being insane and kept him from beating me up or my mother. My mom did what she could to try to remember to make sure that his medication was always on par.

Sometimes in these cases his medication needed to be adjusted, and we couldn't help or control the situation and so, he had to go to the doctor for adjustments. During those periods of time, we discovered that he needed it and from the time that he actually got the doctor's appointment, we experienced some very abusive and crazy times.

I honestly don't remember what was worse getting beat up or watching my mother getting beat up. I think watching my mother getting beat up was worse.

I was often mad at my mother because she didn't stand up to him. I didn't really understand this, it really wasn't part of her personality. My mother tried and every time she did, she got beat up. I on other hand then tried all the time and didn't care if I got beat up, because to me the emotional side was worse than the physical part.

SELF-EMPOWERMENT RESET

I tried to talk my mother into leaving him, not only did she not come from that generation, but she also just didn't have it in her. It really wasn't part of her life lesson or part of her demeanor. Watching someone get abused is very difficult.

My mother spent a lot of her life crying either for me or for herself. My Grandmother became a single mom when my mother was only four years old and my uncle, her brother was not yet born. Her mother was very strong primarily because she had to be but also she had more of that demeanor. I think I am more like her most of the time, more than my mom.

My father was six years older than my mother, who lived down the street from my mom. They actually fell in love fairly young and were on and off for a very long time. This was mostly because my father was very insecure.

This was a result formed because he didn't have anything, and his worth was always connected to the amount of money and the number of things he had. My mother wanted some of that of course but was not driven by that.

SELF-EMPOWERMENT RESET

All of this formed my primary Foundation, until I made a point of changing my Foundation, which took the next 40 to 50 years to overcome. That is how long it took me to understand that I didn't have to have or settle for what was given to me. I do have to say that I was much more driven than my mother. I was much more like my father in that regard.

My father was a stellar employee, everybody loved him everywhere he went. My father was an amazing employee and always did his best. He went above and beyond. He thought about going off on his own, but that just wasn't an option for him. There was just too much fear. I believe in my heart of hearts; this was the reason when I went off on my own and that he tried to discourage me.

It took me an extremely long time to discover that my father actually did love me, he just had a very strange way of showing it. I am also aware that he always wanted the very best for me. He didn't want me to stress the way he did. At the same time, I think he was a little bit envious and also very curious as to where I got the courage to open up my own business. My father never did, so on some level I think that also bothered him.

SELF-EMPOWERMENT RESET

My mother was of course my source of unconditional love, and she was my soft pillow to land on when I needed one. My mother also used to say to me *"just make sure you get married, even if you get divorced its okay, as long as you get married."*

Interestingly enough, that is exactly what happened but not for that reason. I met my husband, and we soon got married. We were extremely happy for a good ten years and then we started to grow apart. This happened after we both spent some time in a war in Croatia.

My former husband saw different things and I saw things different. We came back to Canada, and he had the hardest time adjusting. I don't actually think he ever really fully adjusted. I on the other hand had had enough of the war adventure and it was time to get to work and make up for lost time.

I got a job at the beginning, I then, opened up my own Spa and I loved it. I continued my journey of self-discovery and personal development. As I did that, we of course grew further and further apart. He continued to drink and smoke; like we did when we were kids. I had no desire for that, I kept hoping and praying things would change.

SELF-EMPOWERMENT RESET

I suggested that we go to counseling, and he wouldn't hear of any of this. I did what I could for as long as I could. Then I just couldn't do it anymore! I finally left him; it was shortly after I closed down my business and went to go work at a bank. which couldn't be any more different from my personality.

Shortly after this, I had to file for bankruptcy as everything was in my name. And the worst thing of all, is shortly after this all happened my mom passed away from Alzheimer's. She had spent 7 years in a nursing home with Alzheimer's. All four of these very pivotal turning points in my life all happened within a year and a half. I thought I was going to pass away!

Most of the time I wished I had. One day I had counted the money in my wallet and there was $8 and that is all the money that I had, and I had to decide what I was going to buy for that week I had a dog, was it going to be dog food or was it going to be food for me.

I vowed to myself that I would never be in a situation like this ever again. As you all know by now; the life of an entrepreneur is not always a very linear path it is very squiggly and irregular.

SELF-EMPOWERMENT RESET

We have ups, we have downs, we have circles, we have squares, rectangles, triangles Etc.! And its true I was never there again. This was mostly because I had acquired cushiony credit cards and lines of credit if I needed them. Which I did, several times!

There have been some wonderful times, after all, my life got interesting beyond measure. My father also ended up in a nursing home for the last three and a half years of his life with dementia. Fortunately for me, all the medication made him a nice person and we had a fantastic three years that we never thought that we would have.

I had the honor of being beside his side while he was passing, just as I did with my mother. This did more for my peace of mind, my heart, and soul then most of my life did.

My parents left me a tiny bit of money which I very strategically invested in real estate. I bought myself an investment property. My blueprint father would have been so proud. I did this because in the meantime I had gotten my real estate license and was working as a real estate agent.

SELF-EMPOWERMENT RESET

I was also hired as a recruiter in a Human Resources company. I did pretty good for myself actually. A long time ago when I was in my thirties. I decided that when I hit 50 that I would create some Investments. And so, I did. I did not work for a large corporation, and I wasn't going to walk away with a big fat pension, so I had to take care of myself.

This was my driving force for moving forward. I also discovered that I really loved doing what I do. The issue I struggle with is that I get bored very easily. This keeps me on my own toes, and I have to continuously make my work interesting. I have been doing real estate for a while and had taken a two-year sabbatical from it and then after 8 years I got tired of doing the recruiting and needed a desperate change, which 2020 provided.

I had wanted to work from home for many years and my boss would not allow it. I knew I had to get out of the office environment and that I would be far more productive at home, but I didn't know how. And when in 2020 we all had to work from home this is my opportunity, and I knew that there was no way I could ever go back. I got a coach I took some courses, and I did a major pivot. I went back to doing more coaching,

SELF-EMPOWERMENT RESET

I opened up a Publishing Company and I did Real Estate. This kept me busy for a while I couldn't do retreats, but I could do classes online. In my whole life I never thought I would have a publishing company. English not being my first language, I always struggled with reading I was always a slow reader. And my boss always used to tell me I was terrible at writing. Its true, I am not much for corporate jargon. If I could open a Publishing Company anyone could. In fact, I did a lot of-if I can do it, others can do it!

Needless to say, I had a blast, I did very well for myself, and all of this made me super confident. At age 57 I had finally learned to trust myself fully. In a lot of ways, I had developed a new me and did a lot of ways the true me came out to play. I made a point of adding something new every year.

Every New Years I planned for one or two new things I was going to do that year. I have been doing virtual summits for a few years and quite randomly. And so, one new year I decided that I was going to do one Summit every single month. Just so you know I was terrified! I thought to myself I must be crazy, who would do this to themselves?

SELF-EMPOWERMENT RESET

Who would put themselves under this kind of pressure? Me!! That's who! I literally spent the first 6 months finding my sweet spot in the whole thing. At the end of the 6 months, I did a two-day Summit. I then decided that a one-day Summit for 6 to 7 hours was my sweet spot, and I could totally handle this.

After months and months of reading peoples bios I decided that it was more interesting if I did not read their bios. Also not reading their bios was easier for me and that added to my sweet spot. I then won an award for them, and I was super excited! The company then came back to me and asked me to be a judge and so I did. I love doing new things.

I love doing you things when they work even more. I have spent years Learning from other coaches, a variety of seminars, more books than I could ever count and more tapes and CDs that I knew were even available to me, not to mention YouTube videos.

I learned that the foundation of self- love was the key to everything and that this was my mission, to speak on and to teach others. Whether it was with public speaking, book-writing, or coaching.

SELF-EMPOWERMENT RESET

The beauty of everything is that I went through all of this so I can help others get empowered and show them how to love themselves.

I built up quite a reputation and was the recipient of quite a few Awards and received a lot of respect in my industry. Which made me very happy. I discovered that I love challenging myself. It wakes up my cells and invigorates them in a way I never thought it would.

I am sure my parents are hand in hand with God watching and helping me from above. I know that they would be very proud of me. These are truly words I never thought I would ever say. I believe I can comfortably say that I too am proud of myself. I have created a life that I absolutely love getting up in the morning for to live! I consider myself lucky happy content and confident.

I value integrity, authenticity, and responsibility. All of this coupled with great communication! These are the values I look for in my partners in business and personal as well as my friends and clients. I have very firm boundaries, and I no longer have the trust issues that I grew up with. I truly love honor and trust myself!

SELF-EMPOWERMENT RESET

As always I have future plans, I will be opening up a non-profit this year as I have wanted to do this for well over 10 years now. I have some additional ideas Under My Sleeve too, so stay tuned!

In my life I have had to let go of some very dear people to me. Creating firm boundaries is not always a pleasant feat. It is however a necessary one if you want your vibe to stay high. After everything I can now honestly say I love, honor, respect, and accept myself!!

If I can do it, you can do it. I don't plan on stopping and I don't think that you should either. Always make sure you do what you love. Stay blessed!

~ LOVE AND LIGHT

Rev. Dr. Marianne Padjan

~ Chapter 2 ~

Amanda M. Renaud

Keep Going Goddess!

I remember being a young women working many food service and retail jobs. I often saw many things and circumstances that changed my perspective on business. I remember thinking work should not be this hard and make me feel this way. I often felt like I had no control of my life. I spent many nights often wondering how wealthy people did it. I felt like I was working so hard and not really making any traction in my goals.

I watched the women around me working so hard and raising children and it seemed so difficult for many. My own mom was a single mother who worked very long hours and attended school with four children. My mom also spent a long time struggling financially. Despite the struggle, she made things happen and never gave up on meeting our household needs. I knew from a young age that struggle was always a challenge.

I had also come to the conclusion at around 18, no one was coming to save me. I knew I needed more education and would need more leadership experience.

SELF-EMPOWERMENT RESET

I often felt because I was young, it would be challenging. It reality, it wasn't all that difficult because I wanted it.

I always had a lot of responsibility since I was a young child because I was the eldest daughter, and my mom worked a lot after her divorce. My mother was buried in debt and pain, so she worked a lot. I watched my mom have many sleepless nights and I often admired her relentless work drive.

My mother faced many awful men, and it seemed no matter how much she worked, she could never get ahead and I saw how it changed her. I began working at a very young age to help her and my siblings. I knew I could count on myself, and I wanted to make lots of money and help my family. I grew up surrounded by a lot of poverty and saw the consequence's of poverty, I couldn't stand it. Poverty breeds such negative circumstances. It is the invisible shackles that society ignores.

Large families experience high levels of poverty and it's a lot harder to start life out that in bigger families sometimes. I also found the education around community resources, just wasn't there for most. I had figured out there were many gaps in life, and I would have to be educated and work hard to escape all of that.

SELF-EMPOWERMENT RESET

I had my son very early in life and my educational opportunities would also have to take a bit of a back seat. So, I learned how to be a better leader in the meantime.

I spent many years learning how to manage others and businesses. At 17, I had my first real management job, it came with its challenges.

I would face many different life challenges and have many lie altering experience's that would hold me back quite a bit, including a fatal car accident. I spent some time in a coma and suffered a traumatic brain injury. I would lose myself and this would steal who I was for along time, as it left me with many physical challenges and cognitive challenges.

This meant, I would have to work a lot harder than everyone else around me. I would have to relearn who I was and understand this new brain of mine. I developed very peculiar personality traits, and I would have to manage those as well. I became quite outspoken after my brain injury, and I would then finally get to attend college, where I studied child and youth treatment for four years and exceled in this program.

SELF-EMPOWERMENT RESET

College would help me develop better skills and my leadership skills would be challenged, and I would then become very well versed in human behavior and realise my journey of self healing would begin. My journey would also be full of heart ache, suffering, and loss.

One major life lesson I would have to learn and live was that: Circumstance did not change my life responsibilities. No matter how hard life was or what happened to me, I had to keep going because my children were watching. I knew that I could not count on everyone, because most would fold around me and those were painful lessons to learn.

I knew that I needed to work hard and have goals that were realistic. When people would ask what I wanted to do, I would tell them that I wanted to help other people and write a book about my car accident. I wanted to own a home and be a good mother to my children.

I would end up experiencing many toxic circumstances. That would help me decide what kind of person I wanted to be. I wanted to be someone respected and someone that could help others become the best version of themselves. Of course, after my accident; my mind and body had changed quite a bit, leading to self-esteem issues.

SELF-EMPOWERMENT RESET

I would do many years of therapies and rehabilitation after my accident. I met and worked with some highly respected professionals who taught me humility and compassion.

I would have a lot of growing and self-discovery to do and conclude, that I was different from others. Many people would laugh when I would tell them my goals, especially about becoming a Writer. Many would doubt me and tell me I couldn't do it, even when it came to me attending college. Most assumed because I had a brain injury and the accident, I would never do it, but I did.

I would learn that they did not matter and as long as I could see it in my mind, I could do it and I did become an Author. I did not just become an International Best-Selling Author in 2018, but I would soon become an owner of a publishing company. I had finally worked enough management jobs that would exhaust me for various reasons to finally push me to venture out on my own.

I become Certified in Transformational Coaching and began pouring myself into my business. There was a final moment as I decided I was not going to keep watering myself down.

SELF-EMPOWERMENT RESET

I knew I had something, others did not, self discipline and a positive mindset. I realised that I was actually quite smart even with a brain injury and if I had my own business, I could control my schedule a lot more. I often faced many challenges when it came to support and childcare being a single mom.

It was experiencing toxic people and places nd how it left me feeling. I never wanted to feel that way again. It was the constant betrayals and disappointments that gave me this relentless drive. I remember working a management position and writing my very first solo book. I would get up at three AM, every single day and be at my 9-5 job by 7 AM.

When I started the 3 AM wake ups I also had twin boys who were toddlers. Having twins made me excel at sleep deprivation and I learned the value of actual hard work and time management. Of course, I did experience burn out, prior to opening my business.

The year prior I was served, and another civil proceeding would begin, this time I had someone try and take me for $300,000 dollars and use the legal system to do this. My eldest sons father also passed not long after. There were many challenges that kept coming to me over the years. However, I was still working on my dreams of becoming a Writer.

SELF-EMPOWERMENT RESET

Despite ending up in court again, after a prior seven-year litigation. I felt hopeless. I was reminded again of the pains of loss and left to try and hold my life together. Many times, in life, I have had to rebuild and refocus. I truly believe despite the challenges; I would not be where I am today.

I have learned also that owning a business is hard, but it gave me freedom. Freedom to make decisions and focus on areas of my business that I wanted to improve. Owning my own business has been a liberating journey and I am proud of the brand that I am building and the things I am doing to help others.

I am living all of my dreams finally and proud of the leader and woman I have become. Business is often filled with unique experiences and challenges, but it comes down to a matter of how bad you want something. It comes down to being willing to make sacrifices and ignore the people who do not believe in you.

Not everyone is going to understand your goals, visions, or dreams and that's okay. I believe the challenges of business ownership can be difficult, but it is the people who show up and support you to achieve, that truly matter. Many people won't understand what you're trying to build, and its perfectly okay. Align yourself with the people who do.

SELF-EMPOWERMENT RESET

I also believe that you have to have courage and never let the hesitation in your mind become your leader because hesitation and fear are poor leaders, they are also hindrances.

As a leader and business owner you have to be able to be an excellent problem solver and be willing to put yourself out there. A Goddess never stopes believing in herself, no matter what lays ahead.

Nothing worth doing comes easy and it requires you to stand strong in who you are and never fear failure, rejection, or the word no.

You are going to make mistakes, and others won't see what you're doing. Many wont even support you but the ones who do, always cherish them. I also know you have to love what you do and be proud of it, no matter what.

You have to be willing to have the courage to try. Failure is not something to fear, but rather something to learn from.

Some of the most influential people in the world had to fail and sacrifice a lot to stand where they do. So, when you consider this, it high lights the very essence of how bad you want something.

SELF-EMPOWERMENT RESET

All businesses go through periods of struggle and that's why as a business owner its important that you continue to keep going and work on yourself.

Our insecurities from the past can become our loudest voices but we should learn to drown them out and surround ourselves around individuals who believe in our vision and causes. In business, the difference between someone successful and someone unsuccessful, is someone who didn't give up!

A Goddess doesn't give up and she keeps going despite the challenges and hardships that may arise. A Goddess pours her power into all that comes in her direction, and she uses that power to create beauty and success in the world around her.

Being a business Goddess is never an easy journey, but with dedication, strength, and determination any women can achieve and succeed in the business world. Set gaols, gather resources and supports.

Embrace your authenticity and be bold about who you are. Business requires a relentless drive built on passion and strategy. With the right focus and skillsets, you can shine your light on to the world and make lasting impact.

SELF-EMPOWERMENT RESET

Stand firm in who you are, what you do, and your brand. Women are needed in business more than ever to lead. By encompassing your full potential and hard work, you can own your industry and make changes.

Most people experience some kickback in business or entrepreneurship and give up but will work endlessly for someone else. Build your dreams and do it no matter how hard it may seem, or someone else will.

There are no quick solutions or band-aid formulas. You can not escape the endless hours and dedication it takes to build something worth having and if everyone can have it or do it, you should not want it.

A Goddess recognises that the things she is doing and building are unique and require originality, as well as perseverance.

It is also critical to recognise that you can never control the things taking place around you. You can only control your response and the way you move when things get tough. This is never a precedent to quit or stop trying, it's a call to action to work smarter and harder.

SELF-EMPOWERMENT RESET

Having a strong Network of individuals who are smarter than you is also not a threat, it is a blessing. Being around people who breaking barriers and skilled is a blessing because they can and want to help! Celebrate others and support where you can.

A Goddess does the best with what she has and can make it happen. A Goddess sees value in all around her and does not waste time focusing on "lack" or "deficit." She must focus on all that is working and learn to fill in the gaps even if it means retaining or asking for help. Have no shame in knowing your limits and when to seek help from others.

A good leader and business Goddess understands that we can not possibly have all the answers and looks to others for their wisdom and is ready to embrace a lifetime of learning.

A business Goddess never let's fear lead and stands where they are in humility and grace. You never reach a destination without some planning and unplanned instances. You always have a few choices to make: A continuation, progress, or an ending.

Circumstance will always reveal which choice is best for you. Your character will decide how you wither the rough waters of life.

SELF-EMPOWERMENT RESET

There is no greater feeling than conquering and living your dreams and only a Goddess can fight for visions, dreams, and future. No one comes to save you but you.

Do not ever fear of doing what it takes and the people who won't believe in you, they don't matter. A goddess doesn't have time or energy for anything, that does not align or serve a purpose. Stay focused, ready, and willing. Let the past be a marker of growth, and the future be successful. For all who are brave enough to conquer the fast-paced world of business.

You can do anything you can envision, and there are no barriers too big to conquer. Above all, never forget where you started from and have compassion. A Goddess rules her world and business with the hands of compassion and humility. **Keep Going Goddess!**

~ **Amanda M. Renaud**

SELF-EMPOWERMENT RESET

~ Amanda M. Renaud ~

Amanda is an Experienced Leader with a demonstrated history of working in Sales, leadership, and Entrepreneurship for more than twenty years. Amanda is the CEO of Magnetic Publishing. Amanda a 6x International Best-Selling Author herself. Amanda holds an Advanced Diploma in Child and Youth treatment and has knowledge in Program development, Community services, Crisis Intervention, Business Development, and Customer Relationship Management (CRM). Amanda is a Strong professional who is also a certified life coach and has won numerous Awards in Canada for sales and her writing.

Amanda is a motor vehicle accident survivor who has made immense impact for her herself and the people around her. Amanda has transformed her life into the true definition of success. Amanda also released her first Solo Self development Novel in October of 2023 " Exceptional Minds" a wonderful prelude into her Leadership teachings and upcoming course designed to enhance leadership skills globally.

SELF-EMPOWERMENT RESET

Amanda also became a number one best seller just recently with her newest co-authorship book Luminous Leaders where herself and co- authors share valuable knowledge about leadership. Amanda was presented with a lifetime achievement award recently for her continued work in publishing and contributions to leadership from the Mind Academy Arena.

Amanda continues to focus on serving others, provide quality publishing, and coaching services that are empowering the lives of many globally. Amanda a single mother of three sons. Amanda has faced many hardships throughout her life but despite the challenges, she continues to share her knowledge and help emerging writers face the challenges in publishing and everyday life with her diverse skill set and continued efforts driven by her compassion for writing and serving the people around her.

Lastly, Amanda has released her newest book Love, Lust, & Limerence which is a boom designed to help others with relationships and became a Best-Seller within twenty-four hours in three categories. Amanda continues to make her mark in the publishing industry.

Magneticpublishing2023@gmail.com

~ Chapter 3 ~

Denise Millet-Burkhardt

Business Fostering Kindness, Proactive Listening, Open Communication, and Empowering Women in Embracing the Role of a Goddess in Entrepreneurship

Introduction

In the dynamic and often challenging world of business, embodying the qualities of a goddess can lead to profound success and fulfillment. A Goddess in business is not only a leader but also a nurturer, a visionary, and a beacon of strength. She embraces qualities such as kindness, proactive listening, open communication, and the empowerment of other women. This chapter delves into these essential attributes and explores how they can transform the entrepreneurial landscape.

Treating Others Kindly

At the heart of being a goddess in business is the principle of kindness. Treating others with respect and compassion creates a positive and supportive environment that fosters collaboration and innovation.

Kindness in business can manifest in various ways, from offering a helping hand to a colleague in need of acknowledgement and appreciating the efforts of others.

Kindness is not a sign of weakness but a powerful tool that can build trust and loyalty. When leaders treat their team members kindly, they inspire dedication and hard work. Employees who feel valued and respected are more likely to go above and beyond in their roles, contributing to the overall success of the business.

Moreover, kindness extends beyond the confines of the workplace. It involves being considerate and fair in business dealings, treating clients, partners, and competitors with the same level of respect. By fostering a culture of kindness, a Goddess in business can create a ripple effect that positively impacts the broader community.

Listening Proactively

Proactive listening is a cornerstone of effective leadership. It involves not only hearing but truly understanding and valuing the perspectives of others. A Goddess in business recognizes the importance of giving her full attention to those she interacts with, whether they are employees, clients, or stakeholders.

SELF-EMPOWERMENT RESET

Proactive listening requires being present in the moment, asking thoughtful questions, and providing feedback that shows genuine interest and concern. It is about creating a safe space where individuals feel comfortable sharing their ideas and concerns.

By practicing proactive listening, a leader gains valuable insights that can inform decision-making and strategy. It also helps in identifying and addressing potential issues before they escalate. Furthermore, employees who feel heard are more engaged and motivated, leading to higher productivity and job satisfaction.

Listening proactively also means being open to feedback and willing to make changes based on constructive criticism. It is a continuous process of learning and growing, which is essential for personal and professional development.

Open Communication

Open communication is the lifeblood of any successful business. It involves fostering an environment where transparency, honesty, and clarity are prioritized. A Goddess in business understands that open communication builds trust, facilitates collaboration, and drives innovation.

SELF-EMPOWERMENT RESET

Encouraging open communication means creating channels where information flows freely, and everyone feels comfortable expressing their thoughts and ideas. It involves regular team meetings, one-on-one check-ins, and open-door policies that invite dialogue at all levels of the organization.

Transparency in communication ensures that everyone is on the same page, reducing misunderstandings and fostering a sense of unity and purpose. When leaders communicate openly about the company's vision, goals, and challenges, they empower their team to take ownership and contribute meaningfully to the business's success.

Open communication also involves being honest about mistakes and setbacks. A goddess in business acknowledges when things go wrong and takes responsibility, using these moments as opportunities for learning and improvement. This level of honesty and vulnerability strengthens the bond between leaders and their teams, creating a culture of mutual respect and support.

SELF-EMPOWERMENT RESET

Building Up Other Women in Entrepreneurship

One of the most impactful ways a Goddess in business can make a difference is by empowering other women in the entrepreneurial world. This involves creating opportunities, providing mentorship, and advocating for gender equality.

Supporting other women means celebrating their achievements and offering guidance and encouragement. It involves sharing knowledge, resources, and networks to help them overcome obstacles and achieve their goals. By lifting each other up, women can create a powerful and supportive community that drives collective success.

Mentorship plays a crucial role in building up other women. A goddess in business takes the time to mentor and coach aspiring female entrepreneurs, offering insights and advice based on her own experiences. This mentorship helps women navigate the complexities of the business world and develop the skills and confidence they need to succeed.

Advocacy is another important aspect of empowering women. A goddess in business uses her platform to speak out against gender discrimination and promote policies and practices that support women's advancement. She champions diversity and inclusion, recognizing that a diverse workforce leads to greater creativity and innovation.

Furthermore, building up other women involves creating a workplace culture that values and supports women. This includes implementing family-friendly policies, flexible work arrangements, and initiatives that promote work-life balance. By addressing the unique challenges women face, a Goddess in business ensures that women can thrive both personally and professionally.

Conclusion

Being a Goddess in business is about more than just achieving success; it is about creating a positive and lasting impact on those around you. By treating others kindly, listening proactively, fostering open communication, and empowering other women, a Goddess in business leads with grace and strength.

SELF-EMPOWERMENT RESET

She builds a legacy of compassion, collaboration, and empowerment that inspires others to follow in her footsteps and transform the entrepreneurial world for the better.

~ Denise Millett- Burkhardt ~

Denise Millett Burkhardt was born and raised in Brooklyn, New York, and received a congressional award for her invaluable service to the community. She also received the "Producer's Award" from the Mayor of Los Angeles for being multicultural and making the city a better place to live and work. The youngest woman ever to own an OTT Networks, Denise has given away over twelve million charitable dollars airtime on fourteen Networks, and now has a platform, Traverse TV, which will be a basis for positive reinforcement through music, entertainment, health, nutrition education, and information. All rated PG-14 reaching a global audience. Denise is working on a project to house 30-40,000 homeless Veterans and end the homeless population by the year 2030 by duplicating every program in the State. Very soon, she will be rolling out a K-12 Global Educational Program that will pay students in Crypto Currency to learn and get a better overall education through Satellite Delivery. She will also be launching a Worldwide Tele-Medicine Platform through Satellite Delivery that will provide unlimited options for medical care.

denisemb@traversetv.com

~ Chapter 4 ~

Dr. Andrea Adams-Miller

The Goddess Within: The Brain and Brawn of Her Success and Power

I. Reclaiming the Title of Goddess

Throughout history, women have been the architects of greatness—leaders, creators, nurturers. In ancient times, goddesses weren't just revered; they were feared for their power. Somewhere along the way, society rewrote that script. It is time we reclaim it.

You are more than just a businesswoman. You are a force of nature. A powerhouse. A queen. A Goddess. But for too long, we have been conditioned to dim our light, fearing that stepping into our full power means sacrificing love or acceptance. The truth? The more you rise, the more you attract exactly what you desire.

The Neuroscience of Worthiness

Your self-worth isn't something that needs to be earned—it already exists within you. The challenge is that the brain constantly reinforces past beliefs, often shaped by external validation.

SELF-EMPOWERMENT RESET

If you have ever felt the need to prove yourself repeatedly, this is simply a neural loop that can be rewritten. By understanding how to harness the power of your mind, you can step into a reality where success is inevitable.

Self-worth is more than just a mindset—it is a neural command center. Your brain is constantly reinforcing beliefs about what you deserve. If you have been trained to seek external validation, it is time to rewire the code.

Imposter syndrome? It is a lie. Neuroscience proves its just faulty programming that can be rewritten. Neuroplasticity is your superpower. Train your brain to expect success, and it will seek confirmation.

Self-certainty creates unstoppable momentum. The more you believe you belong, the more the world will agree. Belief in oneself is the foundation of success.

When you cultivate an unshakable sense of self-worth, you naturally exude confidence, making it impossible for others to ignore your presence.

SELF-EMPOWERMENT RESET

Your certainty becomes a self-fulfilling prophecy—when you act as if you belong, people respond accordingly, offering opportunities, respect, and admiration. The key is to trust your abilities, own your expertise, and step forward without hesitation, knowing the world is ready to receive your greatness.

Publicity as a Reflection of Inner Power

How you present yourself to the world directly mirrors how you see yourself. Publicity is more than vanity; it's confidence, trust, and impact. People naturally gravitate towards those who exude certainty. When you fully own your presence, you become unstoppable.

Visibility is not vanity—it is power. Neuroscience reveals that confidence is contagious, and when you own your space, you become magnetic. When you step into the spotlight with conviction, you invite success, opportunities, and high-level connections into your life. People are drawn to those who radiate certainty, and by making your presence known, you set the stage for more significant impact, influence, and recognition.

SELF-EMPOWERMENT RESET

The world takes notice of those who take charge, so claim your space and let your power shine.

Publicity is more than just being seen—it is about being recognized. The more you step into the spotlight, the more your subconscious knows you belong there. When you embrace being seen, you elevate your business and inspire others. Stepping into visibility is not just about gaining attention—it is about making an impact.

The more you show up, the more you solidify your authority, build trust, and create lasting influence. Every time you claim your space, you open the door for others to do the same, creating a ripple effect of empowerment and success.

II. The Neuroscience of Feminine Power in Business

The Role of Emotion in Leadership

Women have been told emotions make us weak. Science says the opposite—emotions make us unstoppable. Our ability to feel deeply, connect intuitively, and lead with empathy is not a liability; it is our greatest strength.

SELF-EMPOWERMENT RESET

Emotional intelligence fuels decision-making, enhances relationships, and fosters resilience. The most successful leaders do not suppress their emotions—they harness them as a tool for influence, inspiration, and transformation. By embracing our emotions, we unlock a level of power and presence that commands respect and drives extraordinary success.

Emotions fuel the best decisions. Leaders who embrace EQ outperform those who ignore it. Empathy builds bulletproof loyalty. Oxytocin, the bonding hormone, is a trust-builder. Authenticity is magnetic. People do not buy perfection. They buy realness.

Taking ownership of our emotions fills our souls and strengthens our leadership. We can navigate challenges with grace and clarity when we understand that emotions are a tool rather than a hindrance.

Leaders who embrace their emotions use them as a guiding force to make better decisions, build deeper connections, and create trust within their networks. Emotional intelligence is the foundation of impactful leadership, where vulnerability is not a weakness but a demonstration of power.

SELF-EMPOWERMENT RESET

By leaning into empathy, authenticity, and self-awareness, we cultivate an environment of loyalty, collaboration, and mutual success.

A D.O.S.E. of Business Connection: What Real Relationships Foster Success is more than just strategy—it is about brain chemistry. The right combination of Dopamine, Oxytocin, Serotonin, and Endorphins (D.O.S.E.) is a dose that fuels success and happiness, keeping you at your peak.

Dopamine fuels momentum. Celebrate wins to create an unstoppable success loop.

Oxytocin fosters trust. The deeper the connection, the stronger the business.

Serotonin builds confidence. Recognize your achievements to reinforce self-worth.

Endorphins sustain resilience. Joy and movement keep your energy high.

Women thrive in connection-based business models. Lean into it. Build networks that feel inevitable, where collaboration is not just a possibility but a natural outcome. The most substantial businesses are built on relationships, trust, and mutual empowerment.

SELF-EMPOWERMENT RESET

When you intentionally create and nurture connections, you expand your opportunities—and you create an ecosystem where success is shared, amplified, and multiplied.

Overcoming Fear: The Science of Taking Up Space

Confidence isn't a personality trait—it is a trained behavior; a muscle that strengthens with every bold action you take. Your amygdala, the brains fear center, is designed to keep you safe, but in doing so, it often holds you back from stepping into your greatness.

The truth is that confidence is not about eliminating fear; it is about acting despite it. The more you challenge those self-imposed limitations, the more your brain adapts, building resilience and self-assurance. It is time to override outdated patterns, embrace discomfort, and take up the space you were born to own.

Cognitive reframing: Flip "I am not ready" into "I am prepared."

Somatic techniques: Power poses are not just hype—they change your biochemistry.

Visualization: The brain believes what it sees. Show your success daily.

SELF-EMPOWERMENT RESET

You send an undeniable signal to the world when you enter your power. Your energy commands attention, your presence shifts the atmosphere, and your confidence becomes a magnetic force. When you embrace your full potential, people listen, doors open, and opportunities align effortlessly. You belong here, and the world is waiting for you to take up your rightful space.

III. Publicity as a Goddess's Throne

The Visibility Principle: The More You Show Up, The More You Receive

Women are taught to be humble—shrink, defer, and wait for permission. Forget that. Boldness builds empires. The women who own their voice, take up space, and refuse to be sidelined shape industries, lead movements, and command respect. Success does not favor the silent; it follows those who dare to be seen and heard. It is time to step forward, amplify your impact, and embrace the unapologetic power that is your birthright.

Authority is built through exposure. The more you show up, the more you are believed.

Your brand is your legacy. Own your story. Tell it with conviction.

Visibility equals credibility. Get seen, get known, get paid.

SELF-EMPOWERMENT RESET

Visibility is more than being noticed—it is about intentionally commanding attention. The more consistently you show up, the more trust you build with your audience. Whether through media appearances, thought leadership, or brand presence, your credibility grows when people see you as an authority in your space. Those who hesitate to be seen often remain overlooked, but those who embrace their visibility reap the rewards of influence, impact, and income.

Media Magnetism: How to Be the Goddess Everyone Wants to Feature

Publicity is not a game of luck. It is about mastering psychology—understanding how the human mind perceives authority, influence, and connection.

How you present yourself to the world determines how people respond to you. It is about crafting the right message, building emotional resonance, and positioning yourself as the go-to expert in your industry.

The most successful people don't wait to be discovered; they engineer their visibility precisely, ensuring their impact is felt and their presence is unforgettable.

SELF-EMPOWERMENT RESET

Confidence is contagious. Mirror neurons make people subconsciously adopt your energy. Stories captivate brains. People do not remember facts—they remember emotions.

Authenticity is non-negotiable. The more YOU you are, the more irresistible you become.

Embracing authenticity is more than standing out—it's fully stepping into your power. When you strip away the layers of societal expectations and show up as your most genuine self, you create a gravitational pull that draws the right people, opportunities, and successes toward you.

Authenticity builds trust, and trust is the foundation of influence. The world craves realness, and the more you embrace who you truly are, the more magnetic your presence becomes.

Publicity Rituals: Daily Practices for Goddess-Level Fame

Building a powerful presence is not an accident—it is a daily practice. If you want to be unforgettable, show up intentionally every day. The key to standing out is not just being seen and recognized for your authentic power and expertise.

SELF-EMPOWERMENT RESET

Morning mantra: I am seen, heard, and celebrated.

Daily visibility habit: Post, pitch, or engage—every single day.

Embody your success. Speak, dress, and act like the icon you are.

Success is more than mindset; it is a full-body expression of confidence and presence. When you carry yourself as a leader, the world responds in kind. Your energy, posture, and self-presentation create an undeniable force that attracts opportunity, respect, and admiration. Every choice—from your words to your wardrobe—should align with the power you claim. When you embody your success, you more than influence people, you command attention and inspire action.

IV. The Goddess of Wealth and Abundance

The Neuroscience of the Money Mindset

Your relationship with money is a neural blueprint—a deep-rooted pattern shaped by past experiences, beliefs, and emotions. Every financial decision, whether conscious or subconscious, directly reflects how your brain has been conditioned to perceive wealth.

SELF-EMPOWERMENT RESET

Let's rewire it for abundance by shifting scarcity-based programming into a mindset of limitless potential. When you align your thoughts, emotions, and actions with financial success, you create a flow where money is no longer a source of stress but a tool for empowerment and expansion.

Scarcity is a script received. Change it or erase it. Money flows where certainty grows. Believe it is yours. Your bank account reflects your self-worth. Charge accordingly.

Money is more than a transactional tool—it is an energetic reflection of how much you value yourself and your expertise. If you hesitate to set high rates, undercharge your services, or feel guilty about financial success, you reinforce subconscious scarcity patterns. The wealth you attract is directly tied to your confidence level.

The more you recognize your worth, the more others will invest in what you bring to the table. Wealth is a byproduct of certainty—own your value, charge what you deserve, and watch abundance flow effortlessly.

SELF-EMPOWERMENT RESET

Aligning Feminine Energy with Wealth Creation

Wealth does not come with force—its about alignment. True financial success isn't a battle to be won but a flow to be embraced.

When you align your actions, energy, and mindset with abundance, opportunities appear effortlessly, and resources come to you in unexpected ways.

This idea is more than working harder; its about working smarter, leveraging your gifts, trusting your instincts, and allowing prosperity to move through you instead of chasing it with exhaustion.

The most successful women do not demand wealth; they embody it. Intuition is a business strategy. Trust it. Energy attracts opportunity.

Elevate your frequency. Passion should be profitable. If you love it, monetize it.

Turning your passion into profit is more than financial gain—its about aligning your work with your purpose. When you build a business rooted in what excites you, you create an energy that draws success toward you.

SELF-EMPOWERMENT RESET

Passion fuels resilience, creativity, and innovation, making it the most powerful driver of long-term wealth. The key is to believe that your unique talents and interests hold real value and to position yourself, so others see that value, too. When you monetize what you love, you no longer work—you thrive.

V. Conclusion: Reclaiming Your Throne

The Final Neuroscience Hack: A D.O.S.E. to Keep Smiling Your brain is constantly processing and reacting to the world around you. How you think, the emotions you cultivate, and your habits shape your success trajectory. Neuroscience shows that Dopamine, Oxytocin, Serotonin, and Endorphins (D.O.S.E.) create the biochemical foundation for resilience, joy, and confidence. By activating these powerful neurochemicals, you can train your brain to sustain motivation, embrace challenges, and radiate positivity—ensuring you keep smiling no matter what life throws.

Affirm your worth—relentlessly. Your brain thrives on positive reinforcement, and a

D.O.S.E. of hope keeps you smiling through challenges.

SELF-EMPOWERMENT RESET

Rewire your brain for unstoppable success.

Make your visibility non-negotiable.

Visibility is the key to influence, opportunity, and success. When you commit to being seen, you position yourself as an authority in your field, a leader others turn to for guidance and inspiration.

The more you show up, the more trust and credibility you build. Your presence is your power—own, amplify, and watch as doors open effortlessly in response to your confidence and consistency.

The Goddesses Publicity Blueprint

Your story, impact, and name are etched in the minds of millions. Your presence is more than a fleeting moment; its a legacy that shapes industries, inspires movements, and transforms lives.

How you carry yourself, how you speak, and how you show up in the world all contribute to how you will be remembered. This moment is yours to step forward, claim your space, and leave an imprint that echoes for generations. Let's make it happen.

SELF-EMPOWERMENT RESET

Call to the Wild: Stepping into Your Divine Influence

The world is shaped by those who dare to own their presence. When you step forward with clarity and confidence, everything around you shifts. Your business, influence, and opportunities expand in ways you never imagined. Now is your moment to act, step into your highest power, and claim the success that has always been yours.

- Write your personal manifesto.

- Commit to one bold move today.

- Own your space. The world is watching.

Stepping into your divine influence is not just about showing up—its about showing up fully. It is about owning your brilliance, embracing your visibility, and walking into every room as if you belong there—because you do. Your business, your brand, and your impact reflect the power you hold within. Now is the time to step forward, take control, and radiate the full force of your goddess energy.

When a woman steps into her power, the world shifts. And that, my dear goddess, is your destiny.

~ **Love, Dr. Andrea**

SELF-EMPOWERMENT RESET

~Dr. Andrea Adams Miller~

Dr. Andrea Adams-Miller: The Powerhouse Behind Publicity, Influence, and Legacy. Dr. Andrea Adams-Miller is her name, but what she is...she's a force—an unstoppable, undeniable, revenue-generating powerhouse.

With a $15 billion Rolodex and a mastery of neuroscience, business growth, and publicity, she transforms entrepreneurs, thought leaders, and industry titans into household names while ensuring they create lasting legacies.

If influence had an architect, Dr. Andrea would be its mastermind.

For over three decades, she has been the secret weapon behind elite entrepreneurs, celebrities, and CEOs who want to elevate their brands, multiply their income, and secure their impact for future generations.

A master of subconscious persuasion, she fuses neuroscience with high-impact publicity, transforming businesses with strategies that captivate, convert, and cash in.

SELF-EMPOWERMENT RESET

What She Offers:

- Publicity & PR Power: Do not just be seen—be sought after. With a strategic media blueprint, Dr. Andrea ensures her clients land top-tier press, TV, and stage opportunities, establishing them as the go-to experts in their fields.

- Neuroscience for Influence & Wealth: She does not just teach influence; she rewires your brain for it. Through neurofeedback, NLP, hypnosis, and subconscious programming, she helps clients break through mental blocks, release limiting beliefs, and unlock their next level of wealth.

- Business Growth & Legacy Building: Scaling is not about effort—it is about leverage. With access to the worlds most powerful networks, Dr. Andrea helps clients create strategic alliances, monetize their expertise, and build empires that outlive them.

- Fractional Chief Connection Officer: Your network is your net worth, and she's the ultimate connector. Whether you need high-value partnerships, investors, or doors opened to A-list opportunities, Dr. Andrea makes it happen.

SELF-EMPOWERMENT RESET

- High-Level Masterminds & VIP Experiences: Success is not just about what you know but who you surround yourself with. Through exclusive, invitation-only masterminds, retreats, and VIP experiences, she brings together the most elite minds to collaborate and elevate.

Why Work with Dr. Andrea? Because she gets results. Period. She does not deal with wishful thinking—she deals with transformations. If you are ready to stop playing small and start thinking, acting, and earning like an industry leader, Dr. Andrea is the ultimate catalyst.

Dr. Andrea has been the publicity architect behind brands that have exploded in visibility, revenue, and influence. Her approach is not cookie-cutter—it is tailored, strategic, and designed for maximum impact. And here is the truth: If you have the vision but haven't figured out how to execute at the highest level... its because you have not worked with her yet.

SELF-EMPOWERMENT RESET

Dr. Andrea turns entrepreneurs into icons, businesses into movements, and ideas into profit-generating machines. The question is not whether you should work with Dr. Andrea Adams-Miller...The question is:

How much longer can you afford not to?

Ready to step into your next level of success?

Contact Dr. Andrea Adams-Miller now at

www.TheREDCarpetConnection.com.

~ Chapter 5 ~

Tammy Williams

Discovering Our Inner Business Goddess Through Life Experience

Being a Business Goddess of something is about attitude and a combination of female and male energies to charge forward. Confidence, knowing your worth, celebrating yourself and loving yourself. Its not about taking the word literally where the ego can work overtime to makes us think we are better than others or where an egotistic energy is felt by others.

I found this out in my twenties, I remember when I was put to the test doing cold call B2B telemarketing. I was eager, nervous, and up for the challenge when I was given the task to start dialing. From interview recruiter to sales to sell temporary staffing services. This entailed me calling 30-40 companies a day that we had not done business with before.

The goal was to secure 10 face to face appointments. It did not take long for me to be overwhelmed and discouraged. I just wasn't used to being told so many times in a day. I remember it like it was yesterday. I felt excited moving into this new role.

SELF-EMPOWERMENT RESET

It became daunting for me I was second guessing myself wandering why accepted this new role. I became so overwhelmed that I actually broke down crying several times.

Thankfully, I had an incredible manager that helped me change my mindset which helped understand it was numbers game and that every no was getting me closer to a yes. She did a great job reminding me of how capable I was a young woman. Within months things turned around for me, my inner Goddess was released by conquering my self doubt.

I can relate to the expression self-doubt will count you out, because this almost happened to me. I had to dig in deep, to find my confidence to keep going. I learnt that you can not have a sale without having rejection.

This is when my journey as a sales professional began. I learnt to focus on my strengths, appreciate my feminine side and use my love for people to share, share and share, which replaced the words sell, sell, and sell. Which is now considered consultative selling.

SELF-EMPOWERMENT RESET

This is taking the approach of working together to find the areas a client would like improvements, has certain needs and the sale professional provide solutions on how to get the desired results. Being seen as more of an adviser, a consultant of sorts not an aggressive, pushy salesperson. It is the latter that has given sales professionals a bad name.

The consultative approach is more about assessing the situations, asking the right questions, listening more pitching less, sharing by informing and educating which sets you up as an Expert to the potential client.

This has become a very important approach since it fosters rapport, allows the sales professional the opportunity to put the potential clients needs first, instead of just pitching your products and services. The consultative approach encourages the mindset shift to the sales process literally being equivalent to a cross country not a 100-meter race.

When you think about sales I am sure you will agree NOTHING happens without it. This applies to a jobseeker, an entrepreneurship, a business owner.

SELF-EMPOWERMENT RESET

This applies everything from being a greeter, a cashier, a receptionist, a single person, a sales representative, a customer service representative, a company sales representative, an independent distributor/contractor, a job seeker, an entrepreneur, and a manager.

Just think about it for a few minutes. Each position listed above is really sales. In textbook fashion sales is described as the exchange of goods or services for money.

Each role is encouraging a buy-in of some kind to evoke various emotions such as: trust, taking stock, being convinced, making a decision to buy, hire and even date.

For Example:

Buy-in of the job seeker based on their resume.

Buy-in by the mom with her children getting them to do certain tasks.

I share this analogy to put people at ease so that they can view themselves as a natural born salesperson that may or may not have had any professional sales training or had a sales job.

SELF-EMPOWERMENT RESET

Another reason to share this analogy is because of the negative connotations often associated with being a salesperson. As a customer or employee many of have experienced various type of salespeople.

Guess what? If you are an entrepreneur, you are a salesperson. A good salesperson is a solution provider, listens to hear and not respond, as well as; adds value.

The Sales Process is a Series of Steps:

- Understand your services/products

- Identify your target audience

- Prospecting by developing genuine connections

- Qualify your future clients

- Know your product/services

- Strategy social media, encourage referrals, emails, direct mail

- Sharing of information, free offerings, samples

- Offer solutions that add value

- Clear messaging with your intro, elevator pitch, and marketing

- The ASK aka The CLOSE

SELF-EMPOWERMENT RESET

Bring your inner Business Goddess out by being 2-3 steps ahead of your customers. Being a business goddess means not giving up or quitting. My mindset changed when I realized as a sales professional every NO, was getting me closer to a yes. When my confidence increased I started looking for the NO's.

Everything comes down to sales. If you are single and open to finding a companion or soulmate. You are a salesperson selling yourself with your overall presentation and with your conversation.

If you're looking for a job you're a salesperson selling yourself on paper with your cover letter and resume. If you work at a greeter at a department store you're a salesperson because you're creating an environment and a space to make people feel happy to repeatedly come into the department store.

This is why I am convinced that everything comes down to sales. Many industries state women are their best salespeople.

Hooray for us! I believe this may be true based on some of the nurturing, insightful, caring qualities that many women have.

SELF-EMPOWERMENT RESET

Tapping into our inner Business Goddess qualities such embracing our femininity and viewing as SUPERPOWER not a weakness! I get immense joy in coaching people on to genuine relationships and how to create customers that create customers.

It can truly be uncomfortable to think of ourselves as a goddess, but I would like to say that we have to dig in deep and know our strengths know our worth and ask for it. This will help develop a powered mindset that will help us to truly be fearless and show up in spaces where people gravitate towards us..

Starting with taking inventory of your skills, what are the skills that you have, and what are the skills that you don't have? Realizing that there is no competition because you are unique and that we are not for everyone nor is everyone for us.

Think of the household appliance manufacturer. Statista www.staetita.com states The Microwave Ovens market worldwide is projected to grow 4.22% (2025-2029) resulting in a market volume of US $11.82bn in 2029.

SELF-EMPOWERMENT RESET

I share this to impress upon you that manufacturers keep developing new designs, and features, regardless of another manufacturer developing a new microwave they do not typically think there is already one out there, so I am not to create another one.

This is BIG business thinking that I believe can be curtailed as Business Goddess thinking there is a big world out there. It so beautiful to really dial in on what your differences are so that you can feel confident in your offerings and what you can provide to people. We need to great at asking for help and using the many AI tools available to assist us.

This will allow us to spend more time on the activities that really lead to growing our networks, spend building those relationships, and connecting with others. Think Globally even if you start locally is key forging ahead.

I would like to leave you with this ....When we feel comfortable using the word Business Goddess we give others the inspiration or even permission to think of themselves as a Business Goddess. Calling yourself a Business Goddess will become more natural when we hang out with people aspiring to win or are winners because you will not feel like you are bragging! Go Business Goddesses Go!

SELF-EMPOWERMENT RESET

~ Tammy Williams ~

Tammy Williams is a wife, mom of 3, still makes her husbands lunch, a 6x International Best-Selling Author, Sales, and Marketing Leader with over 15 years in marketing and sales. She has a passion for helping break the inequalities that women have been faced with a for centuries hence her collaboration as an Advisory Board Member for Camera's for Girl's a registered Charity, Advisory Board Member of International Men's Day Canada, The Founder of Women, Champagne, and Real Estate and CryptoSmart Chicks.

SELF-EMPOWERMENT RESET

Tammy is a firm believes that your health is wealth has led to being a Health Advocate with APLGO and worked in the Diabetes and Auyervada Health sectors. She also believes we all can give, and she started a Walk a Mile in her shoes campaign several years ago and has been able to collect over 443 pairs of ladies new and gently worn footwear which has been donated to various places in Durham region.

Tammy Williams:

tammy@womenchampagneandrealestate.com

https://womenchampagneandrealestate.com/blogs/

https://www.facebook.com/groups/womenchampagnerealestate/?ref=share

tammy_unlimited - Instagram

champagnelivingbytammy

LinkedIn https://www.linkedin.com/mwlite/in/tammy-williams-59b098265

~ Chapter 6 ~

Linda McBee

Empowering Women in 2025: A Vision of Purpose, Prosperity, and Legacy

In today's fast-paced world, the opportunity to transform women's lives through empowerment, purpose, and prosperity has never been more critical—or more attainable. As a business goddess, I have embraced the strengths of visionary leadership, confidence, balance, and mastery to inspire, uplift, and create pathways for women to achieve unlimited income and unparalleled freedom.

For 2025, my mission is to help women achieve not only their financial goals but also the health, experiences, and legacy they've always dreamed of. By enabling women to earn an additional $10,000 a month—and eventually dream bigger to achieve $100,000 or more per month—I aim to ignite a global movement of women living their best lives, exploring the world, and creating generational wealth.

SELF-EMPOWERMENT RESET

Below, I will share the three core ways I am channeling my strengths to empower and bring this vision to life.

1. Transforming Financial Mindsets and Building Pathways to Unlimited Wealth

The first step in empowering women is breaking through limiting beliefs about what is possible in terms of income and wealth. Too often, women are conditioned to think small, settling for enough to get by rather than embracing their potential to create financial abundance. My work starts here: helping women transform their financial mindset and believe in their ability to achieve unlimited income while giving them the tools to do so.

Through mentorship, coaching, and strategic systems, I help women start by creating an additional $10,000 per month. This is the baseline -- foundational income that allows them to pay off debt, invest in their dreams, and reduce financial stress. From there, I challenge them to think bigger and bolder. What if $10,000 a month was just the beginning? What if they could scale to $100,000 a month and beyond?

SELF-EMPOWERMENT RESET

I provide them with practical strategies, like leveraging scalable business models, diversifying income streams, and mastering sales and marketing techniques, to make these dreams a reality.

But financial empowerment is more than just numbers—it's about confidence. I work to instill unshakable self-belief in these women, reminding them that they deserve wealth not only to sustain themselves but to fuel their passions, fund their missions, and change the world. By showing them how to align their financial goals with their higher purpose, I help them create businesses that bring both income and impact, transforming their lives and those around them.

Real Results:

In 2025, my programs have already helped dozens of women cross the $10,000/month mark, giving them the confidence and means to expand their businesses, develop their own teams, and dream on a whole new level. One woman I mentored, for example, turned her side hustle into a six-figure-a-month enterprise, allowing her to leave a toxic corporate job and travel the world while funding a non-profit for underserved girls.

SELF-EMPOWERMENT RESET

2. Inspiring Holistic Success: Health, Freedom, and Exploration

Empowerment isn't just about financial success—it's about creating a life that aligns with one's deepest desires and values. I firmly believe that financial abundance should go hand-in-hand with health, freedom, and personal fulfillment.

My vision for 2025 includes helping women cultivate the vibrant health they've always dreamed of, experience the freedom to travel the world, and check off those bucket-list experiences that make life truly extraordinary.

As a business goddess, I emphasize balance and wellness as essential components of success. Through my programs, I guide women to prioritize self-care and health as the foundation for sustained growth. This includes integrating practices like mindfulness, fitness, and proper nutrition into their daily routines. When women feel their best physically and mentally, they are unstoppable in their pursuit of success.

In addition to health, I empower women to design their businesses in a way that gives them freedom and flexibility. I help them create a life where work and adventure coexist seamlessly.

SELF-EMPOWERMENT RESET

In 2025, I see these women exploring the world, from sipping wine in the vineyards of Tuscany to trekking through the jungles of Bali, all while knowing they have built businesses that fund their dreams.

Real Results:

One standout story is about a single mom I mentored who not only reached her financial goals but also transformed her health by losing 50 pounds and regaining her energy.

She now works remotely, running a thriving coaching business, and recently took her kids on their dream trip to Paris. Her life is proof that holistic success is achievable when women are empowered to prioritize both their business and themselves.

3. Creating a Ripple Effect: Building Legacy and Inspiring the Next Generation

True empowerment isn't just about transforming individual lives—it's about creating a ripple effect that impacts families, communities, and future generations. In 2025, my vision is focused on helping women not only achieve success for themselves but also use their wealth and influence to leave a legacy of empowerment and opportunity for others.

SELF-EMPOWERMENT RESET

For many women, earning $10,000 a month is a game-changer. But earning $100,000 a month or more? That's where the real magic happens. With that level of wealth, women can fund their passions and missions on a scale they never thought possible. Whether it's launching a non-profit, starting a scholarship fund, or investing in businesses that align with their values, I teach women to channel their financial success into purpose-driven projects that create lasting impact.

Legacy is also about teaching the next generation to dream big. As part of my mentorship, I encourage women to involve their families—especially their daughters and sons—in their journey. By showing their children what's possible, these women inspire the leaders of tomorrow to aim higher and embrace their potential.

My programs also include elements of financial education, ensuring that the women I empower are passing on the knowledge and tools needed to build generational wealth.

Real Results:

One woman in my network used her $3,000 initial investment turned it into $3M over the last 3 years.

SELF-EMPOWERMENT RESET

She has honestly taught not only myself but other women in my network to duplicate her actions. Having mentors that instill the secrets to create the vision and working through the mindset needed to dream bigger to better ourselves and leave the legacy we leave for future generations has been unique in my life.

Teaching me to create more action and take more rejection and realize no one else pays my bills or takes care of my family like I do. These stories are just the beginning of the legacy we're building together.

The Vision for 2025 and Beyond

My mission as a business goddess is clear: to empower women to dream bigger, achieve more, and create a life of purpose, prosperity, and freedom. In 2025, this vision is becoming a reality as more and more women join this movement, breaking through barriers and stepping into their power. By helping women earn additional income, prioritize their health, explore the world, and leave a legacy, I am building a global network of empowered, purpose-driven leaders who are changing the world.

SELF-EMPOWERMENT RESET

At the beginning of the year, the word I chose was purpose and did not understand the power and depth of what this word really meant. I am beginning to see it was not just for me but for what I was doing in and through others is the real "purpose."

This isn't just about making money—it's about creating a life filled with meaning, joy, and adventure. It's about showing women that they are capable of far more than they ever imagined and giving them the tools to make those dreams a reality. Together, we are proving that when women succeed, the world becomes a better, more vibrant place.

Key Takeaways for Women Joining This Movement:

- Start by dreaming big but know that $10,000 a month is just the beginning of your journey.

- Prioritize your health and freedom alongside your financial goals to create a truly

fulfilling life.

- Use your success to inspire and uplift others, leaving a legacy that will impact generations to come.

SELF-EMPOWERMENT RESET

As I look toward the future, I see a world where millions of women are living as empowered, financially free visionaries. And the best part? We're just getting started.

~ Linda McBee

~ Linda McBee ~

Linda McBee is an expert in orchestrating unique products and running successful businesses. With an Associates in mental health therapy and a bachelor's in business, she combines her knowledge of human behavior with innovative strategies. Certified in various fields, including Human Interaction Technique and Functional Medicine Coaching, she is passionate about helping others succeed.

Linda has authored multiple international bestsellers and specializes in wellness, drawing from her own transformative journey. Working with coaches, weight loss centers, wellness centers, practitioners, and mental health centers, directing them around health and loving their inner child to be their best version of themselves. Marketing additional products and services to help businesses with solutions and consistent revenue streams. She would love to cheer you on your business journey.

Please reach out to her at

linktr.ee/LindaMcBee

~ Chapter 7 ~

Nicky Cuesta

From Corporate Chains to Entrepreneurial Reign

How I Broke Free, Built My Empire, and Stepped Boldly into My Purpose

If not now, when?

The Day I Knew I Had to Leave, not now when that question echoed in my mind like a drumbeat I could no longer ignore. It wasn't the first time I had thought about leaving, but this time was different. This time, I wasn't just daydreaming about freedom—I was suffocating in the reality of my situation.

   Sitting at my desk, staring at yet another login page. Coming back from a week off after testing my notary commission. Clocked in eighteen of my own scheduled hours and cashed in my first $1600 dollars. I literally had all the evidence I needed to walk away. Why was I still here? Why did I keep proving myself, only to be overlooked?

SELF-EMPOWERMENT RESET

I had spent years giving my all—training, onboarding, leading teams, managing projects—all without the title or the paycheck that reflected my worth. I was the go-to person for answers, the unofficial leader people relied on, yet when it came to promotions or recognition, my name was never called. Was I not good enough? Or was I just too afraid to demand more?

I leaned back in my chair, staring at the screen of my computer that I had no desire to log into. Is this my life? Is this what I'm meant to do forever? The thought of staying in this cycle—of waiting for someone else to validate my worth—felt like a slow death of everything I knew I was capable of.

That's when the fear hit me. If I leave, what's next? How will I pay my bills? What if I fail? But then, another question cut through the doubt—What if I don't? What if I stay stuck in a place that was never meant for me?

I knew at that very moment; I had a choice. I could either let fear keep me chained to a job that no longer served me, or I could break free and build something bigger than me and I made the scariest, most exhilarating decision of my life. I logged in and submitted my resignation letter and walked away.

Building My Empire – The Birth of BALM GLOBAL

I wasn't part of the original plan. In fact, it wasn't even a thought when I first set out on my journey.

In February 2020, I created a YouTube channel called Building a Leadership Mindset. My vision was simple: to create videos that would encourage and motivate people to take a chance on themselves. I wanted to inspire others to step into their purpose, to believe that they had something valuable to offer the world.

But then... it sat.

For two years, the channel collected digital dust. If it wasn't scripted, it wasn't getting done. If my hair and makeup weren't perfect, it wasn't getting done. Perfectionism became my greatest obstacle, keeping me from showing up, sharing my message, and making the impact I had envisioned. Instead of just starting, I let doubt, self-judgment, and unrealistic standards paralyze me.

Still, the idea of Building a Leadership Mindset never left me. I tried again in November 2021, presenting it as a program to an organization that I believed in. I thought this was the moment it would take off. I was wrong.

SELF-EMPOWERMENT RESET

They rejected the idea—not because it lacked value, not because it wasn't good enough, but because of my lifestyle and who I loved. That moment could have shattered me. It could have made me question everything: my purpose, my ability to lead, my worth. For a moment, it did. But instead of allowing the rejection to define me, it became the fire that fueled me. It reminded me of a truth I had been avoiding:

My purpose wasn't meant to fit into someone else's mold. It was meant to break barriers. Then came May 2022—the moment everything changed I met my first publisher, and he asked me one simple but profound question: "What's your story?" I hesitated. Did I even have a story?

That's when it hit me. The seed planted in 2020, the rejection of 2021—those weren't random setbacks. They were catalysts. They were the very moments shaping the journey I was meant to take.

That realization led to my very first book. That book led to my podcast, Building A Leadership Mindset. And finally, in May 2023, BALM GLOBAL was officially birthed into the world. What I once saw as a series of failures was, in fact, a divine setup.

SELF-EMPOWERMENT RESET

BALM GLOBAL was never about perfection—it was about purpose. It was never about approval—it was about authenticity.

Looking back, I realize something powerful: If I had let doubt win, if I had let rejection silence me, if I had waited for someone else to validate my vision, BALM GLOBAL wouldn't exist today. But I said yes to my calling. And that yes changed everything.

Finally Stepping Boldly into My Purpose

Leaving corporate wasn't just a career move—it was non-negotiable. I knew I had outgrown that space, but what I didn't know was what came next. The vision wasn't clear, the path wasn't mapped out, and there was no guaranteed success waiting on the other side. But none of that mattered. What mattered was that I had ideas, passion, and a calling that refused to be ignored. I couldn't shake the feeling that I was meant for more. That the work I was doing—pouring into others, coaching, speaking, writing—wasn't just a hobby or a side passion. It was my purpose.

The only way to make an impact in any capacity was to take action. No more waiting, no more doubting, no more hesitating. Faith became my fuel.

SELF-EMPOWERMENT RESET

I couldn't see the roadmap, but I trusted the One who placed the vision in my heart. I knew God wouldn't give me this calling without equipping me with everything I needed to lead it. And so, I moved—boldly, consistently, and without looking back.

From May 2022 onward, every month became a new level up. Every challenge became a lesson. Every opportunity became a stepping stone. I haven't stopped since that very day.

What I once thought was just a dream turned into a mission. My purpose became clearer with every step—to share the blueprint, help others rise, and guide them toward their own purpose.

Becoming an award-winning speaker and author was never about the recognition. The titles, the accolades, the stages—they were never the goal. The impact was.

It was always about the lives changed, the breakthroughs sparked, and the leaders awakened. It was about showing others that they, too, have everything they need to step boldly into their purpose.

SELF-EMPOWERMENT RESET

And the best part of this journey was assembling the growing community of Ladies of Leadership.

What started as a safe space for a sisterhood—a place where women could share their personal and professional struggles while equipping each other with the tools to shift toward a growth mindset—quickly morphed into something bigger than I could have ever imagined.

It became a movement. A space where competition doesn't exist, only collaboration. a Powerful force of women empowerment where each woman rises, not alone, but together. This was never just about me—it was about us. And the best part?

This is just the beginning.

Five Ways to Overcome Doubt and Step into Your Power as a Business Goddess

Doubt is the biggest thief of potential. It keeps us stuck, second-guessing, and questioning whether we're truly capable of stepping into the greatness we were designed for. But here's the truth: Doubt is a choice, and so is confidence.

SELF-EMPOWERMENT RESET

When I decided to walk away from corporate America, I had every reason to stay—fear, uncertainty, financial security. But I had one greater reason to leave: I was meant for more.

Here are five powerful ways to overcome doubt and step into your reign as a Business Goddess:

1. Silence the Inner Hater by Challenging the Narrative

Doubt thrives in the stories we tell ourselves. I spent years believing that because I wasn't given a leadership title, I wasn't a leader. That because I wasn't being recognized, I wasn't worthy.

That is because I faced rejection, I wasn't meant for success. But here's what I learned: Doubt is just an opinion, and it doesn't have to be yours.

- Ask yourself: What is the real truth?

- Challenge the thought: If I wasn't afraid, what would I do?

- Rewrite the narrative: Instead of "What if I fail?" ask "What if I succeed beyond my wildest dreams?" You are not your doubts. You are your decision.

SELF-EMPOWERMENT RESET

2. Take Action Before You Feel Ready

Perfectionism is just doubt in disguise. I sat on Building a Leadership Mindset for two years because I believed if it wasn't scripted, polished, and perfect, it wasn't worth doing. But the truth is, momentum is built through action, not overthinking.

- Give yourself permission to be imperfect.

- Start now, refine as you go.

- Remember: The people you are meant to impact need your message, not your perfection.

Waiting until you feel "ready" will keep you in the same place forever.

3. Rejection is Redirection—Use It as Fuel

When my idea was rejected in 2021 simply because of who I was, I could have let it break me. I could have let it confirm my doubts that maybe I wasn't cut out for this. Instead, I realized something powerful: The rejection wasn't a stop sign, it was a detour to something greater. Ask yourself: What is this rejection teaching me?

SELF-EMPOWERMENT RESET

- Use setbacks as stepping stones.

- Shift your mindset: "If I wasn't meant for this, I wouldn't have this fire in my heart."

Your vision doesn't need permission—it needs execution.

4. Anchor Your Confidence in Faith, Not Fear

When I resigned from my job, I didn't have a perfectly mapped-out plan. But I had faith—faith that the vision God placed on my heart wasn't accidental. Faith that I had everything inside me to make it happen.

- Trust that the path will reveal itself as you walk it.

- Believe that you already have what it takes.

- Lean into faith, not fear—because fear keeps you stuck, and faith moves you forward.

If God gave you the vision, He also gave you the ability to fulfill it.

5. Surround Yourself with People Who Refuse to Let You Play Small

Doubt cannot survive in a room full of believers. When I launched Ladies of Leadership, I saw firsthand what happens when women come together to uplift, support, and empower each other.

SELF-EMPOWERMENT RESET

Competition disappears. Collaboration thrives. Growth is inevitable.

- Find your tribe—the people who challenge you to rise.

- Cut ties with people who feed your fears instead of your dreams.

- Remember: You are the average of the voices you listen to the most.

Greatness isn't built in isolation—it's built in community.

Final Thought: Own Your Throne

Doubt will always be there, whispering reasons why you're not ready, not worthy, not capable. But you don't have to listen. You have a choice. The day I knew I had to leave corporate, I had every reason to doubt myself. But I made the decision to believe in who I was becoming, not who I had been. And that decision? It changed everything.

Now, it's your turn.

Will you let doubt win? Or will you step boldly into your power as a Business Goddess?

If not now, when?

SELF-EMPOWERMENT RESET

~ Nicky Cuesta ~

Nicky Cuesta is a dynamic entrepreneur, speaker, bestselling author, and the visionary behind BALM GLOBAL—a movement dedicated to empowering women in leadership, business, and personal growth. After leaving corporate America in 2020, Nicky stepped boldly into her purpose, transforming her passion for leadership into a thriving global brand. She is the host of the Building A Leadership Mindset Podcast and the founder of Ladies of Leadership, a sisterhood where competition is replaced with collaboration.

SELF-EMPOWERMENT RESET

A multi-certified coach and community builder, Nicky helps women break free from self-doubt, embrace their worth, and turn their visions into reality. Her journey from corporate limitations to entrepreneurial reign has inspired countless individuals to take risks, rise above challenges, and own their power.

With every book, stage, and platform, Nicky's mission remains clear: to equip, elevate, and empower others to step into their greatness.

Connect with Nicky at:
https://www.facebook.com/nicky.cuesta

~ Chapter 8 ~

Yara Ortiz

From Struggle to CEO: My Self-Empowerment Reset

For the longest time, I believed stability meant a paycheck. A steady job, benefits, a 401(k), and just enough to get by. That's what I saw growing up—a single mother doing her best, stretching every dollar, making it work, even when it felt impossible. I learned early on that financial struggle was a cycle, a never-ending loop that held people hostage, and I was determined to break free.

But life had other plans...

I found myself in a relationship that nearly broke me. Almost 15 years with a man who stripped me of my independence, monitored every move I made, and made sure I knew that my worth was only what he allowed it to be. He controlled my in and out, my time, my relationships—everything. I was practically in jail, serving a sentence, fighting for my sanity, literally. And when I finally found the strength to walk away, I had nothing but my son, my willpower, and my knowledge of finance.

SELF-EMPOWERMENT RESET

Starting over wasn't easy. Fear crept in at every turn, whispering doubts in my ear. Would I be able to provide? Would I ever escape the cycle? Was I even capable of building something of my own? Thankfully, my mom, my dad, and my oldest brother stood by me, giving me moral and emotional support.

Their presence gave me brief moments of relief, like catching my breath before diving back into the deep end. But at the end of the day, the truth was clear—this was all on me. No one else could walk this journey for me. And one thing about being pushed to the edge—it forces you to either sink or fly. And I had no intention of sinking.

Why Nonprofits? Why This Path?

I was able to find a good job with a great salary. But deep down, I knew my purpose was bigger. See, growing up, I saw too many people struggle—not just financially but emotionally, mentally, and physically. They had nowhere to turn. Nonprofit organizations were often their only refuge.

But here's the thing—without proper financial management, nonprofits don't last. They lose funding, they lose resources, and eventually, they disappear, leaving communities without the help they desperately need.

SELF-EMPOWERMENT RESET

I refused to let that happen. So, I took everything I knew—all 15 years of experience in financial management—and I built a business that would serve these organizations. I made it my mission to help nonprofits structure their finances, secure funding, and create sustainability so they could continue to serve. Because when a nonprofit thrives, a whole community benefits.

The Hustle & The Hard Truths

Building a business from scratch as a single mom? No joke. I won't sugarcoat it. There were nights I barely slept, mornings I questioned everything and moments I thought about giving up.

But every time I looked at my son, I reminded myself why I started. I wasn't just building a business; I was breaking generational curses. I was proving that financial freedom wasn't just for the privileged—it was for anyone willing to do the work.

I had to unlearn the survival mindset. I had to believe that abundance was possible, that I wasn't meant to just "get by."

SELF-EMPOWERMENT RESET

And I had to get comfortable charging what I was worth—because for too long, I had been conditioned to believe that helping people meant sacrificing myself. Well, not anymore; that ends now.

Now, let's talk about something real—breaking barriers, setting standards, and navigating life as a woman in business, a single mother, and a survivor of abuse. Society doesn't make it easy for us. We have to fight twice as hard to be taken seriously, to demand respect, and to build something that isn't easily dismissed.

And let's not forget—I'm also part of the Black and Brown community. But let's not even go there right now, because that will ignite a fire where the sun don't shine, and I need to keep writing, but that fight? It makes us stronger.

During this journey, I've had people doubt me. People have undermined me, tried to devalue my work, and questioned my capabilities. And, like any imperfect human, there were moments when their words got to me. Yes, I doubted myself too.

SELF-EMPOWERMENT RESET

But every contract I secured, every nonprofit I helped stay afloat, every woman I inspired to take control of her own finances—that was proof that I was exactly where I needed to be. My work spoke louder than their doubts, and my impact silenced any hesitation I once had.

And let's be real—financial independence isn't just about money. It's about power. It's about choice. It's about never having to stay in a situation that diminishes you just because you can't afford to leave.

The message I want every woman to hear: If you're reading this and you feel stuck—whether it's in a job that drains you, a relationship that breaks you, or a mindset that limits you—I need you to understand something: YOU ARE NOT POWERLESS.

You might feel like you're trapped, like there's no way out, like life has already decided your fate. But let me tell you, that feeling is a lie. You have the power to rewrite your story, to break free, to build something new. It won't happen overnight, and it won't be easy, but every step forward, no matter how small, is proof that you are reclaiming your life. The first step? Believing that you are worthy of something better.

SELF-EMPOWERMENT RESET

I built a business from pain. I turned survival into strategy. I transformed every lesson, every setback, and every hardship into steppingstones toward something greater. I refused to let my past define my future, and instead, I let it fuel me. I went from financial struggle to financial freedom, not because I had a perfect plan, but because I refused to settle. I chose to bet on myself, to learn, to grow, and to keep pushing forward even when the odds were stacked against me. And so can you.

Your reset starts the moment you decide you are worth more. And trust me—you are!

~ Yara Ortiz ~

Yara N. Ortiz is the owner and CEO of Bookkeeping Consulting Services. She is a 2x international best-selling author, award-winning author & speaker, and a successful financial consultant who has helped numerous nonprofits build a strong foundation and structure their financial management systems. With 14+ years of experience in nonprofit financial management, she deeply understands their unique challenges.

SELF-EMPOWERMENT RESET

Yaras perspective is shaped by her lived experiences and upbringing in Puerto Rico and the Bronx, New York. Before establishing her company, she served as the Director of Finance & HR at a charter school in her community.

As a single mom of a teenage boy and a survivor of an abusive relationship with a narcissist, Yara knows firsthand the resilience it takes to rebuild one's life. Her journey fuels her passion for empowering nonprofit leaders with essential financial knowledge and helping them develop robust systems for long-term success.

While Yara specializes in nonprofits, she also serves small businesses and provides personal financial planning for individuals. When she's not hard at work for her clients, Yara treasures spending time with her son, exploring the wonders of nature, or enjoying Zumba sessions.

Linktree link: https://linktr.ee/yaraortiz

~ Chapter 9 ~

Stephanie Brandolini

Hello and Welcome

I've been called to write this chapter for anyone who's ever struggled, or currently struggling with anxiety, self-doubt, imposter syndrome—and everything in between.

Maybe you've felt fear creeping in every time you tried to step into your calling. Maybe you've wondered, Am I really capable of this? Am I enough? I know these feelings well. But what I've learned—and what I'm here to share with you—is that rising isn't about waiting until fear disappears.

It's about moving through it, uncovering the gifts within it, and stepping forward powerfully. But first, let me introduce myself—so we're not total strangers.

My name is Stephanie Brandolini. I'm a multi-passionate writer, storyteller, and creative entrepreneur. Writing has always been my calling, but along the way, I discovered other gifts—leadership, coaching, and speaking my truth in rooms I once thought I had no place in.

SELF-EMPOWERMENT RESET

Today, I stand as a two-time international bestselling author, award-winning screenwriter, and intuitive way-shower in the world of health and wealth. Through my work, I help women and families reawaken their passions, step into their purpose, and go after their God-given dreams. And speaking of God—let's talk about that for a second...

Throughout this chapter, I will be sharing Gods role in my journey. And let me just say, I wrestled with this for a while. I wondered if I should keep it more neutral, more universal, more "acceptable." But here's the truth:

My faith is what got me here. Faith that grew into a beautiful relationship with my Heavenly Father that's given me the strength to rise, to push past my fears, and to write these words for you right now. And the reason I say this with absolute certainty is because God saved my life.

Now, before we get into how to remix fear and rise, I'm being called to share my testimony...

You see, over ten years ago I overcame a severe eating disorder. A prison I was trapped in for fifteen years. It consumed me, controlled me, and nearly took my life.

SELF-EMPOWERMENT RESET

At my darkest point, I was so underweight you could see my heart beating through my chest. And there was one night—one terrifying, pivotal night—when I wasn't sure if I would wake up the next morning. What surprised me was that a part of me actually cared.

Most of me had given up. Most of me was numb, exhausted, done. But somewhere deep inside, I still wanted to live. A part of me that I now know was my true spirit, my soul—the part of me connected to God. And though I had never truly known God at that time, I still somehow knew what to do.

That night, on some kind of strange autopilot, I walked downstairs to my family's library, grabbed the Bible, got back in bed, clutched it to my chest, and started whispering words I had never read before, but somehow knew...

Though I walk through the valley of the shadow of death, I will fear no evil, for Thou art with me...

And OK, I'm going to get extra real here for a second and admit that I kind of, sort of knew this verse from Coolio's infamous Gangsta's Paradise...Regardless, I didn't understand what I was doing. But God did. And He answered.

SELF-EMPOWERMENT RESET

The next morning, my mum had me forcibly taken to the hospital, and trust me, it was not a pretty sight or experience. In fact, I was angry about it for a long time. Until I finally saw the life-saving gift that had occurred and realized how utterly grateful I am for it. It wasn't my will that I am still here. It was God's. He saved me...For such a time as this.

So, when I say I am a woman of faith, I mean it. And I'm not here to push beliefs on anyone. But I also can't tell my story without telling you about the One who saved me.

Maybe you use the word Universe, Source, Higher Power—and that's okay. You are welcome here. And I encourage you to stay open because this is a chapter about rising. Not by ignoring fear or "just letting it go" (because let's be honest, that doesn't work), but by transforming it.

By alchemizing fear into strength, doubt into certainty, and resistance into momentum. Because here's what I believe: Your struggles are not here to stop you. They're here to shape you.

There is gold within the fear, the resistance, the blocks—the very things you think are holding you back actually hold the key to the sacred power within you never even knew existed.

SELF-EMPOWERMENT RESET

And though many people will let fear win and never find it, I'm willing to bet you aren't one of hem. If you're reading this, if you feel something stirring inside you right now, I believe you're meant to uncover the hidden gifts within your struggles.

And in the pages ahead, I'm going to show you how.

Let's begin.

The Pathway to Rising

After recovering from my eating disorder, there was a period of time where I was still so driven by fear, doubt, and debilitating anxiety that I honestly didn't know if there was any hope for me.

I felt trapped in my own mind, stuck in cycles of overthinking and self-sabotage, wondering if I would ever break free. Fearing I was broken beyond repair. But hope was always there.

Hope is a waking dream, a quiet ember that never fully dies out. And in my darkest moments, that still burning spark—the dream of living in freedom, creativity, wellness, and alignment with my true purpose—kept me going.

SELF-EMPOWERMENT RESET

I couldn't always explain it, but I know now that what I was searching for, what kept me alive, was something much greater than me. I found something beyond my own strength—a power that catalyzed me to greater heights than I could have ever imagined...

The grace of God.

Through many struggles, trials, and failures, I discovered something unexpected: The very things I thought made me weak were actually my greatest strengths in disguise. When I stopped resisting and instead leaned into my challenges, while also leaning on God, uncovered a process—a system—that allowed me to:

- Transform fear into fuel
- Shift doubt into clarity
- Turn resistance into momentum
- And so much more...

That system is what I'm sharing with you today.

Introducing the A.F.E.R. System

SELF-EMPOWERMENT RESET

This system is designed to help you move through fear, not around it. This isn't about bypassing your struggles or pretending they don't exist. This is about transforming them into power.

Each phase builds upon the last:

- A - Awareness & Acceptance
- F - Face & Look Beneath
- E - Embrace & Heal
- R - Rise in a Rebirth of Excellence

And they all work together in a cycle of growth.

Let's begin where all transformation starts...

A - Awareness & Acceptance: The Power of Stillness

Most women I work with are already highly self-aware. They recognize when something isn't working. They can pinpoint their fears. But awareness alone isn't enough. Because awareness is uncomfortable. It's that moment when you realize you're stuck in a cycle—like a hamster on a wheel, running but going nowhere. You see the problem, but you feel trapped in it. That discomfort? It's actually your push forward.

SELF-EMPOWERMENT RESET

But first, you get to stop resisting where you are and step into Acceptance. Acceptance: Be Still and Know Here's where most of us get tripped up—we want to rush ahead, have our breakthroughs, and move on.

I know this because I've done it.

For years, I resisted stillness. I wanted to be moving, achieving, fixing, breaking free...I didn't want to sit with the discomfort of where I was. But every time I rushed ahead, I missed something crucial. Because true growth happens when we pause.

"Be still and know that I am God" is a verse that's helped me immensely through this.

Stillness is not passive—it's an active choice to surrender. It's trusting that even in the fear, even in the struggle—you are exactly where you're meant to be, and most importantly, God is with you. There's a vital tool to finding acceptance by the way, a simple one we use everyday without even thinking about it. That tool is breathing.

Accepting what you've been afraid to see in yourself can be overwhelming, triggering anxiety to take over. When this happens we often forget to breathe. Our thoughts race, our bodies tense, and we disconnect from ourselves.

SELF-EMPOWERMENT RESET

So, let's breathe and reset. Seven is a spiritual number—symbolizing completion, alignment, and divine rest. So, let's use seven-count breathing to bring stillness and presence into this moment.

1. Breathe in for 7 seconds.

2. Hold for 7 seconds.

3. Exhale for 7 seconds.

Do this for three rounds.

Feel the shift.

No need to fix anything. Just be here. When you allow yourself to fully accept this moment, fear begins to lose its grip. And in this stillness, God meets you.

F - Face & Look Beneath: Meet Yourself and Uncover the Wound

This is where things get interesting. You've accepted that this fear exists—and now, it's time to face it. This is where stillness will help you immensely because most of you will want to run.

Fear has a way of triggering that fight-or-flight response—the urge to distract yourself, move on, push it away, or freeze. However, God didn't give you a spirit of fear, but of power, love, and a sound mind.

SELF-EMPOWERMENT RESET

So instead of running, I encourage you to stay. Close your eyes. Look at this fear in your mind's eye. If your thoughts start racing, bring back your breath. Breathe in for seven, hold for seven, exhale for seven. Let that stillness settle in. And when you're ready, look beneath it. Because fear is rarely about what we think it is. The things we think we fear most—rejection, failure, not being enough—is usually a reflection of something deeper.

A part of us that was wounded long ago.

A part of us that never fully healed.

And that wound?

That's where God is waiting to meet you.

If you stay in stillness long enough, you'll begin to sense the part of you that's reacting to this fear you're facing. When I've done this, I've often found a child-like version of myself. And let's be real—sometimes, she's throwing a tantrum.

You know the one. The part of you that's screaming, This isn't fair! or I can't do this! Yeah, that's her. But instead of silencing her, listen. Instead of dismissing her, see her. Instead of running away, stay. Keep looking beneath. Beneath, beneath, beneath.

SELF-EMPOWERMENT RESET

Until that part of you—the scared, fragile, younger version of yourself—stands still enough to face you too.

That's when the real work begins.

E - Embrace & Heal: The Power of Compassion

Now, embrace her.

The part of you that has been afraid. The part that has carried the weight of this fear for so long.

Accept her fully.

In your mind's eye, visualize embracing her. She might struggle at first. She might not trust that you're really here for her. But hug her anyway. And as you do, imagine God embracing you both.

You are, He whispers, I have always been with you. Visualize any burden she has been carrying—falling away. Like debris that no longer serves. Like a shroud of shadows, she has outgrown. Watch it fall away.

And what remains?

Just her.

Whole. Seen. Loved.

SELF-EMPOWERMENT RESET

Let her come into stillness with you. It might take time but when she does, she will hug you back. And in this moment, healing begins. This step is rarely a one-time fix.

If you're anything like me, you may have suppressed this part of yourself for years. Maybe she's afraid you'll do it again. So, trust must be built. Come back as many times as you need. Hold her. Speak to her. Let her know that this time, you're not going anywhere. Because the more you embrace her, the more whole you become.

R - Rise in a Rebirth of Excellence

Now, you are ready to rise. But you can only rise with her. The part of you that carried the wound—she is your key. Because within the wound she carried lies the very gift that was meant to be found. Think of an oyster. The grit, the irritation—it's all been there, shaping something precious.

Now, the pearl is ready. And so are you. As you embrace her, feel her merging with you. Not separate. Not something you need to "fix" or "manage." But part of you. Let her dissolve into you, like mist absorbed by light. Because she is no longer your wound—she is your power. And together, you rise. Not just in strength, but in faith. Not just in confidence, but in divine identity.

SELF-EMPOWERMENT RESET

Not just in success, but in the purpose God has ordained for you.

Final Reflection: Your Rising Moment

Take a moment to write (or voice record) the answer to this:

- What gift did I find within my wound?

- How does it feel to rise with this part of me, instead of against it?

Let the words flow freely.

There is no right way to rise—only your way.

But know this:

You were never broken.

You were never lacking.

You were always meant to rise.

And now?

You have.

Closing: Your Rise is Just the Beginning

What you've just experienced is a brief introduction to the A.F.E.R. System—a process that goes far deeper in the full program. This is not just a transformation. It's a way of being.

You are meant to rise—again and again.

SELF-EMPOWERMENT RESET

I would love to hear how this process went for you, feel free to connect with me via the link in my bio. And if you're ready to deepen this journey and rise even higher, let me know. Because your dreams are waiting. And so is God.

With love,

Steph Brandolini

SELF-EMPOWERMENT RESET

~ Stepanie Brandalini ~

Stephanie Brandolini is a two-time international best-selling author, award-winning screenwriter, speaker, and coach from Vancouver, British Columbia, Canada. After graduating from film school, Stephanie worked her way up in the visual effects production world, gaining in-depth knowledge of the TV and film industry. Through her success and spirituality, Stephanie discovered a deeper calling to go all in on her writing and creative gifts to serve others through doing what she loves.

Now, as a creative entrepreneur, she is on a mission to help driven individuals and families break free from the matrix, uplevel their health and finances, get their time back, and build a legacy. All while creating and collaborating on writing, film, and speaking projects that uplift, inspire, and transform audiences worldwide.

Connect with Steph at:
www.stephaniebrandolini.com

~ Chapter 10 ~

Bethany Stone

To Thrive

I was born with an entrepreneurial spirit; it was modeled for me from a very young age. My father emigrated to America at the age of 19 with a degree in horticulture and a desire in his heart to achieve the American Dream. My Father came to the United States speaking four languages, none of which were English.

He decided to serve a mission for his church in hopes of learning English and was assigned to Texas, where he learned Spanish fluently, along with some English, mixing it with some "Spanglish" and "Swissican."

By the time he finished his mission, he looked up my mother, who was also in the U.S. They had known each other as children because their mothers were friends. He would drive three and a half hours to see her, even though she was engaged to another man. That did not stop him.

He continued to drive to see her weekly and eventually proposed to her, despite her engagement. She broke off her engagement and married him.

SELF-EMPOWERMENT RESET

Life was not easy. They were poor and lived in a small trailer. He would teach ski lessons during the day and milk cows at night. He never gave up on his dream and soon was able to open a small landscaping business.

Plants for landscaping are quite expensive if you buy them already grown, so we built a greenhouse where my parents would plant seeds to grow into plants for landscaping.

All of us children were involved; we played in the dirt, watered the plants, and watched the miraculous transformation of seeds into thriving plants. We worked together as a family, and as a child, I didn't see it as work—I thought it was fun. What child doesn't want to play in the dirt? Swiss Precision Enterprise.

This company was started in 1982. There were many ups and downs, and at times my parents were stretched so thin that they had to take on extra work. To provide for all seven children. But they persevered.

I am grateful to have had the opportunity to observe this firsthand; it served as an example in my life. Today, my parents employ nearly 50 employees and service about a 60-mile radius with a successful greenhouse, nursery, landscaping business, and home repairs.

SELF-EMPOWERMENT RESET

My dad is now at retirement age, with my two brothers taking over the family business. It has been an amazing adventure, filled with trials and successes.

Having observed this, I knew that starting my own business would not be easy. I anticipated ups and downs, as well as trials and successes, but I was willing to take that risk.

Like my father, I was born with a deep sense of ambition and drive. As a younger child, I was often found on the soccer field, in school musicals, or competing in ballroom dance. I graduated from high-school early and entered an excellent program that taught speed reading and required a literature paper due at the end of every week.

By the age of 17, I finished my Montessori certification degree and was ready to start my internship. I moved away from home and out of state, began my internship, and truly loved teaching. It filled my soul and felt like my calling on Earth.

At 19, I got married, and a couple of weeks before my 20th birthday, I had my first son. The first year of marriage was blissful. We decided to open a business together—an auto repair shop. While I continued teaching, I would go to the shop to manage the books and ensure everything ran smoothly.

SELF-EMPOWERMENT RESET

However, my husband was dealing with an undiagnosed mental illness and began to self-medicate with drugs and alcohol. He often came home upset and angry, sometimes disassociating. I often found myself on the receiving end of his anger. The situation escalated to the point where he held a gun to my head.

This was a time in my life when I felt I was losing myself. I hid things from friends and family because I didn't want anyone to know what was happening at home. My only drive was to protect my children and keep a smile on my face when they walked into the room.

We stayed married for ten years. I had three little boys with him, but I felt completely broken after the marriage ended. I didn't know how to pick myself back up. I was diagnosed with battered wife syndrome and PTSD; for a long time, just smelling alcohol would send me spiraling into anxiety.

There were times I would have to abandon my grocery cart in the store because a smell would trigger complete paralyzing anxiety. In this weakened state, I quickly became prey to another abusive man. He was physically and mentally abusive, an attorney who emotionally abused me to an unimaginable extent.

SELF-EMPOWERMENT RESET

I felt crushed into dust and as if I could be blown away at any moment. Between physical or emotional abuse, I would choose physical, as it ends quickly. Emotional abuse plants a disease in your heart that spreads and grows, causing continual suffering until you believe the negative thoughts and words.

During my second marriage, I felt incapable of functioning, having allowed this man to poison me, to take over my spirit. I often thought that the world would be better without me. Lying in bed, I considered the pills that could end my pain when I happened to glance outside the window.

As a Montessori educator, I understood a lot about plants and animals. When I looked outside, I saw two hummingbirds building a nest. Hummingbird nests are difficult to spot; they're made of grass, moss, and soft materials. The softest materials that nature has to offer. The nests blend into their surroundings.

Watching this miracle unfold, I realized I had forgotten who I was. I had forgotten that I am a person of value, descended from a strong lineage of hardworking individuals capable of overcoming adversity.

SELF-EMPOWERMENT RESET

Witnessing those hummingbirds inspired me to reclaim my identity and engage in activities that fulfilled me, reigniting my resilience and determination. I began to write, exercise, and cook, activities that brought me joy.

As I grew stronger and more assertive, my newfound independence was not well-received. Being in law, my husband knew the right things to say to maintain control. However, during an encounter with police at our home, an officer discreetly told me that I was being abused. They removed him from the premises, allowing me to take everything I wanted and leave the house. I did so and never looked back.

The momentum I gained from watching those hummingbirds continued to grow within me. I became that determined 17-year-old again.

I recognized my need for stability—for myself and my children—and I moved back home to manage my parents' greenhouses. It was a healing experience. During that time, I opened a private school and taught ballroom dance lessons, worked as a waitress, donated plasma, and took on every side hustle I could imagine.

SELF-EMPOWERMENT RESET

My drive was to improve our lives. Similar to building an electric dog fence, I thought I was creating protective boundaries for myself. In reality, I was confining myself from opportunities I could not yet see.

After these experiences, I felt a strong aversion to men, focusing entirely on my children and my work. In our small farming community of about 1,000 people, well-meaning individuals often tried to set me up on dates. Although I went on a few, they reinforced my belief that men were terrible.

While conducting my side hustles, I occasionally took on clients for private ballroom dance lessons. One day, a man contacted me through Facebook, asking if I taught Blues dancing. Assuming he was an older man, I agreed to teach him. I was surprised to find he was not old at all, about 6 years older than me, and as we danced, he expressed interest in going to other dances together.

We got to know each other, and he expressed interest in dating me. I initially resisted; he shared that he was falling for me. I quickly told him he was mistaken—if he was falling for me, he clearly hadn't dated enough women, as I was not the one he was looking for.

SELF-EMPOWERMENT RESET

Thinking I had freed myself from his pursuit, I was surprised when he messaged me again four weeks later, stating he had dated 42 women and chose me. His strategy as an analyst showed through, and I finally agreed to a date.

God has a unique way of teaching lessons. It was the best first date I'd ever had—an escape room followed by ice cream. He supported my teaching and would often have dinner with my boys and me at my parents' home. Eventually, he proposed, and I said yes.

However, due to my past trauma, the first six months of our marriage were challenging. I spent a lot of time re-evaluating the boundaries I had erected. I had to overcome my fears to fully embrace the growth and vulnerability that come from a supportive relationship.

We have been married for almost six years now. He remains the same kind, loving man who takes me dancing, supporting me and my three boys in every way possible. I have also supported his two boys and a little girl, especially his oldest, who is neurodivergent. This situation has been advantageous, as I specialize in working with neurodivergent populations.

SELF-EMPOWERMENT RESET

I also support each of his children as they need. I am currently teaching Ballroom and am his Daughters Ballroom Dance coach. Funny how things work out.

About two years ago, one of my sons became severely ill, a life-altering condition. He transitioned from an active cross-country runner to needing assistance moving from his bedroom. After numerous tests yielded no answers, a geneticist finally diagnosed him with a mitochondrial variant affecting his muscles. My husband researched ways to help him cope and recover, while I continued teaching amidst the challenges.

Last year, when my husband was asked to return to the office, we faced a difficult decision. Ultimately, I sold my school, leaping into faith and opening my own coaching practice. I have since acquired six additional certifications on top of my 22 years of experience as an educator.

My family is my top priority, but I also thrive on productivity. I work from home while the kids are at school, always available if my son needs me, while still supporting and teaching others, fulfilling my God-given gift.

SELF-EMPOWERMENT RESET

Throughout life, we undoubtedly face leaps of faith, trials, and the necessity of vulnerable moments. Growth is often uncomfortable, and the only way we can advance is by embracing this discomfort and being willing to take risks while accepting potential pain.

Life is not meant to be all sunshine and roses. While it's essential to find the silver lining, one cannot see the rainbow without first enduring the storm. You can't grow beautiful flowers and thriving plants in your garden unless you're willing to get a little dirty. The mighty tree cannot stand strong unless it has weathered the storms and allowed its roots to grow deep.

I am living proof that miracles happen, forgiveness is healing, and life can significantly improve when you open yourself to vulnerable and uncomfortable growth experiences.

Take a moment to evaluate the fence you have constructed around yourself. Are there elements holding you back? Is your fence positioned where you want it, or do you need to push through to reach the other side? Yes, you may encounter shocks along the way, and yes, it will be difficult. But pushing through that boundary will lead to immeasurable and untapped growth.

SELF-EMPOWERMENT RESET

Do not view your challenges as defining or limiting; instead, see them as building blocks that support your development and enhance your capacity for growth.

Consider them opportunities for adaptation and change; sometimes, a shift in plans can lead to even better outcomes than you may have anticipated. The secret to navigating all of this is ensuring that you are continually filling your cup. Take care of yourself, engage in activities that bring you joy, become comfortable with your identity, and strive daily to be the best version of yourself in all your relationships. When you do this, the doors of opportunity that will open before you will be countless.

SELF-EMPOWERMENT RESET

~ Bethany Stone ~

Bethany Stone is a master mindset and life skills coach and the founder of Thriving by Nature. With over 22 years of experience, she specializes in helping individuals develop resilience and personal growth through essential life skills such as persistence, organization, and time management.

A passionate speaker and podcaster, Bethany draws from her own journey of overcoming adversity to inspire others to embrace their potential. She believes that, like seeds, we all can flourish when nurtured in the right environment. Dedicated to fostering growth, Bethany empowers her clients to lead fulfilling and meaningful lives.

Email - bethany@thrivingbynature.com

~ Chapter 11 ~

Kylee Leota

The Way of the Goddess in Business

"The question isn't who is going to let me; it's who is going to stop me." – Ayn Rand

What does it mean to be a goddess, particularly in life and business? How do you embody this presence in a way that is both powerful and relevant to today's world?

Throughout history, goddesses have shared common attributes: strength, courage, compassion, and resilience. These qualities, once revered in mythology, remain just as crucial in modern business.

If you asked people about me, some might say I'm strong, tough, and formidable even. Others might describe me as loving, compassionate, and deeply caring. Some might even say I'm superhuman or super direct. Some people may give you a mixture of all of the above.

The truth is all of these descriptions of me are accurate depending on the context. That is the paradox of being a goddess in business.

SELF-EMPOWERMENT RESET

It is not about being one thing; it is about embodying harmony. And harmony requires the coming together of all of you. Just like in an orchestra, all the sections are needed create the beautiful symphony. At times, some parts will play softly in the background, like toughness, whilst compassion is playing a louder solo, other times, strength will take the lead role.

It doesn't mean those other parts stop playing, but the beauty in the symphony is when all sections play in harmony with each other. This embodiment of the whole self allows the goddess to create her own symphony in life and business. I really struggle with the word "balance," as it implies a static state, but I do believe that success comes from aligning with your true self while maintaining adaptability and agility.

My business journey, like my life, has been a continuous process of reflection recalibration, and evolution. We talk endlessly about authenticity, but the reality is that many of us wear masks—hiding parts of ourselves that we believe are not welcome in business. These masks hold us back from reaching our full potential.

SELF-EMPOWERMENT RESET

The statistics are sobering: 60% of businesses fail within the first three years, and 65% don't survive beyond a decade. So how do you ensure that you're not one of those statistics?

"She remembered who she was, and the game changed." – Lalah Delia

As a single parent of three children with 100% care, launching a business at the height of the COVID-19 pandemic in 2020, I could easily have been one of those failures. But my journey did not begin there.

I have faced adversity that could have easily defined me—but instead, I chose to rise above it. Well may be more accurately, I chose to not let it define me.

I have survived domestic and family violence, endured health scares that left me wondering if I would be able to be a value add to my children, rather than a burden, and navigated the immense responsibility of raising three children on my own.

Each challenge brought me to the brink, but each also forged an unshakable resilience that became the foundation of my business success. We need to remember that we are stronger than we give ourselves credit for.

SELF-EMPOWERMENT RESET

"Do not go where the path may lead, go instead where there is no path and leave a trail." – Ralph Waldo Emerson

Becoming a business owner is not easy, nor is it a guaranteed path to success. It is, however, a path to liberation. To build something in spite of life's circumstances is to reclaim power over your own destiny. I made this decision after the realisation that I was not walking in alignment with my true and authentic self by staying in the "job" I had. Every obstacle I have faced has taught me profound lessons—not just about business, but about leadership.

Leadership is not about having all the answers or never facing hardship; it is about facing the storms, adjusting your sails, and moving forward anyway. It is these Leadership lessons that have empowered me to walk into my true goddess self, and be the author of my own story, rather than a character in someone else's.

"I am not afraid of storms, for I am learning how to sail my ship." – Louisa May Alcott

So how do you uncover your unique ingredients to step into your own power as a modern-day business goddess?

SELF-EMPOWERMENT RESET

If you explore the history of goddesses, you'll find varied interpretations. While some emphasize beauty, a closer look reveals far more: they were warriors, strategists, creators, and protectors. They were strong yet compassionate, fierce yet nurturing.

The idea that you must choose between strength and kindness, or strategy and empathy, is outdated. True power lies in integrating these qualities seamlessly. This is how I approach leadership and business—loving my clients fiercely, championing them, and protecting their growth while also challenging them to rise into their greatness.

Tasha Eurich speaks about the necessity of having "loving critics" in your life—the people who support you wholeheartedly while also holding you accountable to your highest potential. Unlike unloving critics who nitpick or uncritical lovers who praise without substance, loving critics push you to be better because they believe in you.

Every goddess needs these people in her corner. Goddesses leave legacies that last thousands of years. People still speak of their influence, power, and wisdom. How do you create a lasting impact in business, life, and leadership?

SELF-EMPOWERMENT RESET

For me, it has been through eight key pillars that I created called INFINITE Leadership that I use daily to remain formidable in business and life while staying aligned with my true self:

1. **Identity** – Knowing who you are beyond the roles you play is critical for success in business.

As women, we are often conditioned to fit into predefined roles, but true success comes from shedding outdated narratives and stepping into our strengths, values, and zone of genius.

When you own your identity with confidence, you set the foundation for authentic leadership and influence.

Ensuring that the identity you have is the one you created, rather than adopting someone else's narrative of who they believe you should be is imperative. As is the understanding that you have far more power than you give yourself credit for, and if you do not like your current identity, YOU have the power to change it.

SELF-EMPOWERMENT RESET

2. Nurturing – Business success is not just about strategy; it is also about emotional intelligence. Women in leadership must cultivate emotional agility, understanding their own emotions and those of others. When challenges arise, the ability to respond rather than react sets apart great leaders. By nurturing yourself, your team, and your business relationships, you build sustainable success.

3. Fearlessness – Fear will always exist, but moving through it with confidence is what separates successful women from those who remain stuck.

Fearlessness is not about the absence of fear but about confronting it head- on and taking decisive action. Women in business must cultivate the courage to take risks, ask for what they are worth, and create their own opportunities.

4. Innovation – Women are natural problem solvers and creators. Innovation is not just about technology or new products; it's about thinking differently, challenging the status quo, and bringing fresh perspectives to business.

SELF-EMPOWERMENT RESET

By embracing creativity and innovation, female entrepreneurs and leaders can carve out new markets and redefine success on their own terms.

5. Nobility – True leadership requires humility and integrity. Women who lead with nobility understand the importance of removing ego from decision- making. They prioritize impact over accolades and service over self-interest. By leading with authenticity and purpose, they create trust, loyalty, and lasting influence in their industries.

6. Influence – Influence is one of the most powerful tools in business. Women who master communication, develop psychological safety in their environments, and lead with empathy become forces of transformation. Influence is not about control—it's about inspiring and empowering others to believe in their potential and take action.

7. Transformation – Growth requires continuous evolution. Women in business must be willing to adapt, learn, and grow at every stage of their journey. Whether through mentorship, ongoing education, or stepping outside of comfort zones, transformation is the key to staying relevant and thriving in an ever-changing business landscape.

SELF-EMPOWERMENT RESET

8. Ecosystem – Success is never achieved in isolation. Women who cultivate strong networks of mentors, peers, and supporters create opportunities not just for themselves but for others as well. Building an empowering ecosystem allows female entrepreneurs, business owners and leaders to navigate challenges with resilience and create sustainable, long-term success.

Each day, I assess where I am in alignment with these pillars. Where am I thriving? Where do I need to recalibrate? The way of the goddess is not a fixed state—it is an ongoing journey of self-mastery and evolution. *"You may encounter many defeats, but you must not be defeated."* – Maya Angelou

I did not choose the adversities that shaped me, but I did choose how I responded to them. I chose to take control of my story, to turn my experiences into lessons, and to build something greater than myself.

Business is not just about financial success; it is about leading with heart, about showing up when it's hard, and about creating something that outlives you. To walk this path is to defy expectations, to forge your own way in business, and to create an impact that lasts far beyond your lifetime. That is the way of the modern business goddess.

~ Kylee Leota ~

KYLEE LEOTA

ELEMENTS 4 SUCCESS

Kylee Leota is the founder and Chief Vision Officer of Elements 4 Success - a global organisation delivering transformational experiences to individuals, teams, and organisations. Earl Nightingale defines success as "the progressive realisation of a worthy goal or ideal."

SELF-EMPOWERMENT RESET

Kylee wishes to empower people of all ages so that they can develop the confidence, skills, and tools they require to live a life of their design and purpose. She believes that you have the knowledge within yourself to create success and gives you the right tools in your toolbox to help you make these goals and ideals, reality!

As a lifelong learner and educator, she has taught all ages and stage and sectors of schooling including guest lecturing at tertiary level. Kylee consults to and works collaboratively with, Psychiatrists, Psychologists, and other professionals to create sustainable behaviour change for her clients in her coaching role.

"I'm here to accompany you on this journey, providing support, inspiration, and guidance as you strive towards your most meaningful goals. Join me on this transformative journey together, celebrating every step forward as a testament to our shared commitment to personal and professional excellence." Kylee is also the author of the INFINITE Leadership

~ Chapter 12 ~

Rosemary Ghiz

The Power of Unconventional Thinking! Awakening the Goddess Within.

What is a Business Goddess, what it isn't is someone who necessarily excels in her career, but a leader who moves with purpose, intuition, and intelligence. For decades, women have been conditioned to believe that to be successful in business requires some degree of toughness and strong ambition. Truth is that a woman's natural intelligence, and creativity are a far more valuable asset in business, which does not necessarily come through social education but through the people you associate with.

Money has always been a sensitive subject for women and many of us were raised with limiting beliefs and it was not a subject to be discussed around the dinner table. These beliefs definitely hold you back. Most women and I would never discuss finances, and most women don't ask about where things were financially.

SELF-EMPOWERMENT RESET

We didn't know what their habits, beliefs and values were and were afraid to even ask. Were my beliefs and values around money and finances aligned with his? To shift into a powerful money mindset, we must identify and challenge the beliefs that do not serve up and even ignore the nay sayers with the opposing beliefs.

I was born into business and while other children were learning about traditional career paths of pursing a job, I was absorbed into the world of entrepreneurship, where self sufficiency, independence wasn't just encouraged but expected.

Business was in my family and our way of life. Watching my family and extended family navigate the highs and lows of business ownership instilled in me a deep sense of resilience and ambition.

I didn't just learn about business, I lived it. Through the years, as I grew and built my own adventures and faced challenges head-on, I discovered something profound: being a successful businesswoman isn't just about strategy and execution, its about embracing the goddess within.

SELF-EMPOWERMENT RESET

The span was generational, and I didn't know anything different. I thought it was the way things were. Running businesses, negotiations, problem-solving and the drive to create opportunities were as natural to me as breathing. I grew up surrounded by a large family of entrepreneurial business owners and professionals and was put to work in my father's business from an early age. This was my reality, we worked hard and learned from our parents to be strong and resilient. A trait that I carried for most of my life.

My earliest memories are rooted in the hustle and bustle of my family's restaurant, where I served customers, observed as my parents managed operations, and learned the value of hard work, firsthand. My father not only owned a restaurant, but also managed apartment buildings, juggling multiple ventures with a seamlessness that left a lasting impression on me.

We are taught to be handy with repairs and not to depend on others for this. My father loved looking at real estate and took me along on many of these sites and taught me what to look for in a property.

SELF-EMPOWERMENT RESET

My grandparents and extended relatives were no different, they too owned businesses, each with their unique flair and approach, reinforcing the belief that entrepreneurship wasn't just an option but the norm. Its funny though about entrepreneurship, it was not a word I was ever accustomed to or ever used. It was just a way of life.

It wasn't until I stepped into the "real world" that I realized my upbringing was anything by the norm. While I was taught to see possibilities, others saw risk. Where I sought innovation, others clung to security.

While I grew up with one set of beliefs, I learned that there were as many with very different beliefs. Mostly based on the way they were taught growing up.

A book that resonated for me was Robert Kiyosaki's book on his own up *bringing "Rich Dad Poor Dad,"* focusing on the difference based on his own father vs his friend's father with opposing beliefs and values around education and money. The mindset that had been second nature to me was suddenly met with skepticism and at times outright criticism.

SELF-EMPOWERMENT RESET

Thinking outside the box wasn't always welcomed and often judged as unrealistic and that I was not good enough or smart enough to achieve such ambitious goals. I often had conversations with my father who with his wisdom told me that I could do anything I set my mind to achieve. I just needed to figure out a way to make it work.

It became difficult for me being faced with conflicting beliefs and values. It caused me to question and second guess myself. Was I wrong to hold these beliefs in this way, that I wasn't good enough or should I conform, take the safer route and blend into the mold that society deemed acceptable. I felt like I was betraying myself by focusing on trying to fit in and not rock the boat, so to speak.

Listening to the nay sayers that kept telling me not to go down that road and I was not good enough or smart enough was hard to swallow.

I was built to create and constantly thinking big picture was my strength. It was the way I was brought up. I was big on coming up with concepts and ideas to grow but it was not always appreciated or accepted.

SELF-EMPOWERMENT RESET

It took me a long time to realize, but often when I presented big picture ideas and had them crushed before me, was really in many cases a reflection of their own believes and values and their own insecurities about thinking in this way. In some cases, I believe they felt threatened by my eagerness and enthusiasm. I discovered this in my own marriage, that we had opposing beliefs and values that caused much conflict.

Growing up, I witnessed firsthand the resilience required to run a business. I watched my father, and uncles handle the unpredictable nature of restaurant and business life, balancing the daily demands, while simultaneously overseeing his real estate investments. I was immersed into this lifestyle, long before I understood the meaning of entrepreneurship.

A business goddess doesn't follow a prewritten script, she writes her own. She doesn't wait for permission to pursue her vision; she builds it with her own hands and surrounds herself with like minded people. Being around negative people, I've discovered only bring you down to their level of thinking. Some people just like to see you down and failing, likely because they can't do it or won't take the risk themselves.

SELF-EMPOWERMENT RESET

For decades, women have been conditioned to believe that business success requires adopting masculine traits, toughness, and relentless ambition. This was not view by society as attractive, but the truth is, our natural strength as women, intelligence, adaptability, creativity are some of the most valuable assets in business.

Yes, breaking away from conventional thinking comes with challenges, judgement, doubt, and sometimes failure. But it also comes with the freedom to innovate, to lead, and to shape the future on her own terms.

Today, I no longer look at my upbringing as different, but more of an advantage and to take pride in. It gave me the ability to challenge social norms, take the risks, and trust in my own instincts, allowing me to navigate business in ways some others can't.

I've learned that success isn't about conforming to what is expected, its about daring to redefine what's possible.

To the women who have ever been told they think too big, dream too boldly or challenge too much, know that this is your power.

SELF-EMPOWERMENT RESET

The world needs more Business Goddesses, unafraid to break the mold and build something extraordinary. If that makes us unconventional, then so be it. I've learned that we were never meant to just fit in, we were meant to lead and carve our own path.

SELF-EMPOWERMENT RESET

~ Rosemary Ghiz ~

Rosemary Ghiz –Mortgage Expert, Trainer, Speaker and 3X Best Selling Author and over 25 years of experience helping Canadians achieve their home ownership dreams Her vast industry knowledge, combined with her passion for empowering clients, has made her a trusted advisor in the mortgage financing and real estate space.

From first time buyers to seasoned homeowners, Rosemary specializes in guiding clients through the complexities of financing, ensuring they make informed and confident financial decisions.

Rosemary Ghiz – Licensed Mortgage Professional, DLC, Expert Financial

rosemary@rosemaryghiz.ca 647-207-7768

~ Chapter 13 ~

Karen Hewitt

From Chaos to Clarity

One of the most common hallmarks of a great business goddess that we hear about is her creativity and, at times, the double-edged sword of attributing masculine traits to her—such as stoicism, leadership, and control in meetings.

Can we take a minute to address the vast, inflated balloon in the corner of the room? That feeling of being overwhelmed, having chaotic mental states, and feeling as if there are lists so long that you don't know if you will get everything done. I know for myself that this was common.

I had so many business projects and always added something else to the pile. Hyperfocus would kick in, and everything would revolve around that one piece of information.

I want to share this vulnerable part of my life because there were many moments where being a mom, a business owner, a network marketer, and a volunteer in nonprofits left me feeling like an imposter.

SELF-EMPOWERMENT RESET

Maybe this is something that crosses your mind! We look at fantastic role models in different professions, and we wish we were like that, but we claim not to be as good as them.

I would sit at my computer screen, over 100 tabs open in 3 windows, several deadlines around the corner, and then get a text asking if I had finished something else. My brain had everything there, but it just wasn't putting itself into action; it was almost like I was paralyzed. Sound familiar?

I knew I wanted to do more, and I knew I wanted to do things differently, yet all these good ideas swimming around my mind would constantly make me stop and list so many negative thoughts I associated with it.

I was unfocused, untalented, introverted, and shy...the names I would call myself were unending. If you have ever had a moment where you had an idea and then shut it down, then this chapter is for you!

I am going to share my story of how I turned chaos into clarity, as well as give you steps that you can put into action.

SELF-EMPOWERMENT RESET

Before that sneaky thought of being a Neurodiverse, or as I call it, Neuro Sparkly Goddess/Entrepreneur being a negative skill set sneaks in, let me share some famous entrepreneurs that have coined this aspect to build their success: Richard Branson, Barbara Corcoran, Jo Malone, Steve Jobs! You can probably search for so many more.

Our challenges can lie in overstimulation, burnout, time blindness, organization, perfectionism, and even that all-or-nothing cycle that our hyperfocus loves. What this can mean is that what we have considered the stereotypical way for a successful business owner to work are skills we don't have, the systems, the organized setup, keeping to deadlines and even emotional dysregulation.

While this isn't meant to be a chapter where we talk about diagnosis, this is a chapter where I encourage you to look at what your strengths are instead of your perceived weaknesses.

Barbara Corcoran has publicly said that her challenges opened her to creativity that built her success, and Richard Branson has said his dyslexia meant he learned how to delegate.

SELF-EMPOWERMENT RESET

The day I decided to reach out to see if maybe I had ADHD turned out to be a stepping stone on a journey that changed my life. It turns out ADHD isn't my only sparkly friend, and I am ADHD.

On hearing that something clicked in my brain, I wasn't broken or incapable; my brain is just wired differently, and I had to start building a business in a way that works with my brain instead of against it. Plus, women are underdiagnosed or undiagnosed at an alarming rate. I was told for many years that I just had anxiety and needed to get over it.

So, I spent over two decades fighting my ADHD, thinking it was just an anxiety issue that I had to overcome. Stop thinking you have to break yourself to win! Think about how your brain and body best adapt to your business; you are in control of your life, and this is why being a business owner works for you! You need to stop listening to how you are meant to do it and forge your path!

Focus on your creativity and out-of-the-box thinking; this is what makes you a powerhouse in areas such as marketing and branding.

SELF-EMPOWERMENT RESET

Once I realized that was something I was doing differently, I studied the why and found out that being authentic and sharing stories instead of being a carbon copy of someone else. This also led to me becoming a Harvard Business School Certified Disruptive Strategist, as I did not realize that what I was doing with Marketing was what companies have done with expansions.

Look to your hyperfocus as a gift; take those deep focus moments to your advantage. If you see that you are going down that rabbit hole on a business item, let yourself. Give yourself a reasonable time frame to work on it because your brain may be unearthing something that will make your business explode. Set that timer for a couple of hours and see what happens.

Before you say anything, if a couple of hours derails your business entirely, this is a sign to hire more people. What you see as challenges are actually strengths; more now than ever before, authenticity is a key component to a magnetic leader, seeing their journey, success, and even pitfalls.

You are a strong business Goddess, and you need to view yourself that way. Take your strengths, and even if they are not what we have been told are strengths, embrace them.

SELF-EMPOWERMENT RESET

Now I know I have been telling you it is okay to suck at some things because they are not your strength, or it may seem like that. What I am really telling you is that you need to find hacks or a way to overcome them. The day I learned to use software and apps and hire the right people became a game changer in my business.

The first thing I did was list all my struggles in being a business owner and find flexible systems that helped me overcome these. Such as using project management software to list all my tasks, one that works with my calendar to make sure I am not over-committing. I tried many of them before landing on Sunsama.

I also started over-booking my schedules on purpose. Not add more to it, but if a task would take me 20 minutes, I said it as a 30-minute task on my software, knowing I would get a million ideas, and Sunsama gave me a very encouraging message that told me I had scheduled 40 hours in one day, should we look at what's on the schedule?

This also taught me the skill of saying no and not feeling guilty. Looking at what I have on my plate and looking to see if its beneficial helps, as well as allows me to evaluate whether an idea is valuable to my business or not.

SELF-EMPOWERMENT RESET

Most neurotypical entrepreneurs need somewhere to do their work, but someone with the sparkles needs to make sure our working environment matches our energy to work. One of the things I did was make my working environment pretty and pink.

When we feel comfortable and welcomed in our space, it encourages us to spend time there. I even added a heated blanket so I could help regulate my body temperature quickly.

I also made my office space functional with a sit-to-stand desk, a criss-cross chair, and a walking pad. Knowing that when I am overstimulated or frustrated, walking or standing to work helps balance my brain to be more efficient. And yes, my chair is pink, and my walking pad is rose gold just because it is pretty helpful. I added automation everywhere that made sense to me.

With neurodiverse challenges, it is often the little steps that get missed, so adding the automation so its not even a second thought, truly helps. And finally, I recommend setting up external accountability; this can be done in a couple of ways.

SELF-EMPOWERMENT RESET

First, I have an amazing Executive VA that is very much my right hand, checking emails, editing, managing teams, etc., and secondly, I have a long-term accountability partner. We meet every week and have three projects and a BHAG (Big Hairy Audacious Goal) that we share and our progress on each of these.

Having this external report system as an entrepreneur helps with being able to process deadlines and stretch ourselves; we tend to tell each other when we are over or under-setting ourselves for success.

You can also join a mastermind or hire a coach but do something where you are accountable to someone other than your clients.

I realized that my brain did not work the same way as others, despite the fact I had been trying to force it to work that way. It was the day I realized the amount of stress I was putting myself under. Normal is overrated; what Is not overrated; is authenticity.

You don't have to do it the same way as everyone else, or as all the books say! You get to write your success story your way, in your terms, and it will be just as powerful if not more than someone else's.

SELF-EMPOWERMENT RESET

The world does not need another cookie-cutter business leader. It requires you—bold, brilliant, and uniquely you.

SELF-EMPOWERMENT RESET

~ Karen Hewitt ~

Karen Hewitt, born in England and now living in the USA, is a top social media strategist, Harvard Business School Certified Disruptive Strategist, and network marketer. A mom of five, she balances family and career with ease and a healthy dose of sarcasm.

As a member of the LGBTQIA community and a neurodiverse individual, Karen brings a unique perspective to her work. With a loving and compassionate nature, she fosters authentic connections and builds strong relationships.

SELF-EMPOWERMENT RESET

Karen advocates against discrimination and hate, believing in kindness and respect for all. She creates a supportive, inclusive community through her expertise, helping others achieve their goals in social media and network marketing.

LINK www.BlossomtoSuccess.com

~ Chapter 14 ~

Ivy Perez

A Business Built on Belief: My Story of Self-Trust and Success

"The entrepreneurial journey is more than you think"

Little did I know this entrepreneurial journey was to ultimately lead me to discover who I am and who I came to be in this world; to let go of what wasn't serving me and become the highest version of myself; to remove the masks, to be called back to the kingdom of God, and yes, to become a Business Goddess and serve with my heart for the highest good of all concerned.

There were two significant moments later in my entrepreneurial journey when I knew I needed to step into something bigger for myself. One was being asked to build a network of entrepreneurs in my state of New Jersey for a well-established businessman in the entrepreneurial space.

SELF-EMPOWERMENT RESET

The perks were great, and I gave it great thought. Although I was honored, I said no. I said no to that opportunity because I knew I wouldn't be able to give 100% to the business. At that moment I knew I was growing as an entrepreneur, as a woman, as a leader in my own right because up until that point I would say yes to opportunities even if I knew they weren't in alignment…I was afraid to say no.

The second occasion was when I was offered an opportunity from one of my clients (my cleaning business), to work for the family which included 5 homes. This was a tough one. The "offer" was very good, but I knew my work, my thoroughness, and my meticulousness called for more than was being offered. When this opportunity was off the table so to speak, I knew it was my time to design a business that was well known in my community.

A business that would shine above the others because it was designed and created for transformation. More on this later. My entrepreneurial journey began in my early 30s. At that time, I had moved from Brooklyn, New York to Phoenix, Arizona. I had always worked in a corporate environment, but I wanted more for my life.

SELF-EMPOWERMENT RESET

I remember thinking to myself that I didn't want to say, "I work for" but that "I am a…." I was told I would be a fantastic real estate agent because I was gregarious and enjoyed being around people.

I never thought of real estate in any capacity but when I looked into it, it sounded fascinating and I would get to say, "I am a" not "I work for," but in actuality it still was the same thing …." I am a realtor working for ABC Company," even though I was an independent contractor.

It was during this time as a realtor however, that I learned the concept of "serving over selling" via mentorship. I learned about finding out what was most important to the buyer or seller, because many times there was a deeper reason for wanting to sell or buy a home other than wanting a bigger house or downsizing.

That was one of many entrepreneurial endeavors I embarked on. Later in my transformational coaching endeavor I learned about my spiritual nature and this human experience I was having.

SELF-EMPOWERMENT RESET

My life shifted. Building a Business and Overcoming Doubt

The struggles in building in the online space was a bit daunting. I was trying to learn and understand all the things - marketing, funnels, sales, landing pages, groups, communities, memberships, and all the various social media platforms. It was too much. I was spread thin and going nowhere fast.

Around this time a friend reached out and told me of an event that she had gone to in California and all she could think about was how she can see me in this work. Prior to this event, for decades I was challenged with alcohol, so I invested in myself and went through a rigorous transformational coaching program.

During this program, unbeknownst to me, I was slowly being transformed. Two months after I earned my certification I let go of alcohols grip for good.

Although I had a transformation, I was now at my green growing edge of my own personal growth and building a business. There was overcoming doubt, fear, newly surfaced limiting beliefs, imposter syndrome and so much more.

SELF-EMPOWERMENT RESET

Entrepreneurship is at its best is Self-development. I've come to learn a handful of things in this journey:

1. Your journey is yours and yours alone. You have a gift inside of you. Your responsibility is to figure that out and do everything you can to become it, hone the skills, grow, learn, and serve. This all takes time. It can be years, even a decade or two.

2. Your humility will open doors. The question is will you be ready or not. I've had many doors open for me. I either was afraid to enter, or here the big one, I didn't believe I deserved the opportunity. I was always gracious and many times accepted opportunities so I could show up differently for growth purposes.

3. Vulnerability. Man, this is a big one. I learned that being vulnerable is a power not a weakness. Not to be used with ill intent but to show up more authentically, which opened arms.

By being authentically me, I made incredible friendships and bonds along the way. By being authentically, me, the business partnerships and clientele I have attracted to me has been no short of just incredible.

SELF-EMPOWERMENT RESET

4. Love. What love for me was personally being called back to building a relationship with God, which has opened my heart to being more loving and forgiving to myself.

The Transformation

Know that "transformation" can happen in a moment in time, when you DECIDE to change, do something different, or not do something anymore. Transformation comes when you follow your heart or souls calling. When you follow that pull for something greater than yourself. What you are doing is allowing yourself to grow, and you are giving yourself permission to succeed by becoming the best version of yourself.

The day I decided to own my worth came from a business opportunity that I let go off. I mentioned this in the beginning of this chapter pertaining to my cleaning business. Before this opportunity I was in a place where I was doing fine in my business but in all transparency I was in a rut. I was feeling burnt out. Shortly thereafter I came to the realization that I am very good at what I do, that I take care of my clients homes with love and care.

SELF-EMPOWERMENT RESET

Suddenly, it was as if a wave of calm washed over me, and at that moment I embraced my gift. I never looked at cleaning as my gift. Serving from a higher place wasn't in my bandwidth yet.

Approximately 2 years prior to this moment, I began my spiritual journey, and when I embraced my gift, I truly felt Gods presence.

Everything changed from the moment I realized that I am a multifaceted entrepreneur. What I do is; help women build self trust and confidence through daily success habits.

As I love to share my journey of health, exercise and overall, well being - mindset, movement and simultaneously training for my triathlons.

I guide women in breaking through self doubt and creating momentum in their personal growth through my daily Lives where I impart stories, insights, and wisdom on all things personal growth. I contribute to mastermind groups, and I also share my journey of sobriety on multiple platforms to inspire and empower others.

SELF-EMPOWERMENT RESET

I've written about my story of addiction and sobriety in six anthologies, this is number seven.

Currently I'm in the process of writing my own authority book. And.... I run a high-end cleaning, organizing and decluttering business where I bring order, serenity, and peace into people's homes.

This is when I truly realized I was more than an entrepreneur, that I am more of a mentor, leader, and inspiration. Helping women most especially feel seen and heard is important to me and I do it in a variety of ways. This took me a very long time to get and understand when it comes to my gifts. This is how my work transforms others.

As I come to the close of this chapter, I want to leave you with some actionable steps and thought-provoking questions that you can immediately work on to gain insight and clarity.

SELF-EMPOWERMENT RESET

How To Serve Others

Please understand that you do have a gift - something you do so naturally that you overlook its value. The key to confidence, self-trust, and success isn't found in looking outside yourself. It's in paying attention to what you already do well and allowing that to be your foundation.

Your success is a process of paying attention, listening, and building your awareness muscle. Over time you will get better, and you'll come to realize what you do have that is your gift.

You don't need permission to start. The most successful businesses are built step by step, not in a single leap. What matters is that you show up, serve with excellence, and stay committed to your vision—even when no one else sees it yet, or, if maybe you fully don't see it yet. That's how trust is built—first in yourself, then from others. You don't need to have it all figured out.

So, from my heart to yours, from one goddess to another, I want to impart some steps for you to think about and thought-provoking questions to really dig deep.

SELF-EMPOWERMENT RESET

Step 1: Pay Attention to What Comes Naturally

- What do people always come to you for?

- What skills do you take for granted because they feel effortless?

- What problems do you love solving?

For me, it was cleaning and organizing in a way that made people feel cared for. I didn't just clean homes—I created a sense of peace and order. I also helped women recognize their value and feel better about themselves.

Step 2: Say YES Before You Feel Ready

- Start where you are with what you have.

- Take the first opportunity that aligns with your strengths.

- Confidence isn't a prerequisite; it's a byproduct of taking action.

I didn't wait until I had a full business plan—I said yes, then figured it out along the way. Maybe it's time to say yes to you. Just start!

SELF-EMPOWERMENT RESET

Step 3: Serve with Excellence

● Do more than expected.

● Care about your work like it's your own brand (because it is).

● Show up with consistency and integrity, and trust will follow.

Going the extra mile not only turned clients into advocates, but it also turned friends who know me and know my heart into raving fans, and that truly has built my business.

Step 4: Price Your Worth Own It

● People pay for the energy, care, and expertise you bring, not just the service itself.

● Don't undercharge because you doubt yourself.

● The right clients will see the value you bring.

When I stopped second-guessing my prices, I attracted people who respected my work. This step took me a long time, to not just get, but truly understand from a spiritual aspect. Selling your products or services is serving from a place of love because it is …. your gift.

SELF-EMPOWERMENT RESET

Step 5: Never Stop Evolving

- You will never have it all figured out, and that's okay.

- Be open to shifting, growing, and improving.

- Success isn't a destination—it's a mindset.

Every stage of my business brought a new lesson, and that's how I kept expanding. Remember, we are created to expand. It's why we desire, want more, pulled to be, have more and do more.

I will leave you with one last highly calibrated question: WHAT WOULD YOU LOVE?

Final thought...building a business isn't just about money—it's about becoming the woman who believes in herself enough to create something from nothing. That is power. That is trust.

That is success. I wish you love, peace, and great success.

Ivy Perez,

Your Personal Growth Girl

If you have any questions, I am more than happy to support you in any way I can. The best place is in Facebook messenger. I kind of live there!

~ Ivy Perez ~

Ivy Perez is a mom, former marathoner, triathlete, and a passionate advocate for mental health and overall well-being. She is an author, speaker, and firm believer in the power of dreams.

Her certification in Transformational Life Coaching was the catalyst for her own profound transformation—breaking free from a three-decade struggle with alcohol.

SELF-EMPOWERMENT RESET

Now 6 1/2 years sober, Ivy deeply understands the feeling of powerlessness, the desire for change without knowing how, and the doubt that change is even possible. She helps others build trust and confidence in themselves through mindset shifts, movement, and simple daily success habits.

Ivy's mission is to uplift and guide individuals toward mental, emotional, and physical well-being, drawing from her personal journey of sobriety and endurance sports. With compassion and authenticity, she inspires others to believe in themselves and their potential.

In addition to her work as a speaker and coach, Ivy hosts daily "Cawfee Tawk Lives," where she shares actionable insights and tools for personal growth and self-development.

She is in 6 anthologies and currently working on her own authority book. And... when she's not doing all that, she has a high-end cleaning and organizing company.

~ Chapter 15 ~

Olga Geidane

The Power of Alignment—From Survival to Sovereignty

In 2009, I arrived in the UK with no money, no knowledge of the English language, and no idea how I would survive. I had a little boy who depended on me, and failure was not an option.

Beyond the desperation of survival, there was something deeper guiding me—an unshakable knowing that I was meant for more. That knowing became my anchor. I didn't just want to build a life; I wanted to create a reality where I was free, powerful, and capable of guiding others to that same liberation.

This journey wasn't just about learning a language or earning money; it was about rewriting my identity. I had lived most of my life in Latvia as a shy, insecure girl, doubting my own worth and feeling like an outsider in my own story.

SELF-EMPOWERMENT RESET

But moving to a new country gave me an opportunity that few people ever truly take: the chance to become someone entirely new.

I wasn't just surviving; I was aligning with the woman I was always meant to be Resilience became my new normal.

Resilience is not simply about enduring hardship.

It's about using that hardship as fuel to transform. There were nights when I cried myself to sleep, overwhelmed by loneliness as a single mom and fear. I could have let those emotions define me, but instead, I transmuted them into lessons.

One of the most profound realisations I had was this: every time you overcome fear; you gain power.

The fears I faced—speaking a new language, making mistakes, failing, being judged—were all invitations to step into a higher version of myself. The more I leaned into those fears, the more I realised they were illusions.

So how did I went from survival to sovereignty?

SELF-EMPOWERMENT RESET

Here are the steps that I have taken, and I hope these lessons will serve you, too my darling:

1: Change Your Internal Language Before You Change Your External Reality

Most people try to change their circumstances before they change themselves. But I learned that reality is a mirror—it reflects who we believe we are. When I told myself, "I am strong. I am capable. I am here to create something extraordinary," my actions naturally followed. The world responded to my new energy.

If you want to change your life, start by changing how you speak to yourself. Words have frequency, and the ones you repeat internally shape your reality. I used to say, "I can't," until one day, I started saying, "I will." And then I did.

2. Alignment: The Power of Purpose

Resilience carried me through the struggle, but it was alignment that truly changed my life. I wasn't just working to survive—I was working to step into my divine purpose. I have always been passionate about spirituality, growth, and intuition, and as I aligned more with these aspects of myself, doors opened effortlessly.

SELF-EMPOWERMENT RESET

Most people chase success by running after external things—money, titles, recognition. But alignment works differently. When you align with your soul's purpose, success chases you.

When I began living from this space, people started showing up in my life who needed guidance, healing, and empowerment. I wasn't just helping myself anymore; I was lighting the way for others. That is the true power of alignment—it makes you unstoppable because you are no longer just working for yourself. You are moving in harmony with something far greater.

3. Let Your Struggles Guide You to Your Purpose

The very things that challenge you the most contain the key to your highest purpose. I used to wonder, why was I shy? Why did I have to struggle so much? Now, I see that my struggles were my training. Because I knew what it felt like to be powerless, I became passionate about empowerment. Because I had to find my voice, I became dedicated to helping others find theirs.

Look at your greatest challenges—they are not here to break you. They are revealing who you really are and what you are meant to do in this world.

4. Intuition: The Divine GPS

One of the most life-changing decisions I made was to trust my intuition. When I first arrived in the UK, I had no logical plan. I didn't speak the language, I had no financial safety net, and I had a child to support. But something inside me whispered: Go. This is the path.

Many people ignore these whispers because they seem illogical. But intuition is not about logic—it's about alignment. It is the language of the soul, the divine GPS that always knows the way.

The more I trusted it, the more miracles happened. Every time I followed my intuition; I ended up in exactly the right place at the right time. Every time I ignored it; I found myself struggling.

5. Intuition Speaks in Energy Before It Speaks in Words

Most people wait for a "clear sign" before they trust their intuition. But the truth is, intuition speaks in feelings first. If something feels expansive, exciting, and aligned—it is your path. If something feels heavy, constricting, or forced—it is not.

SELF-EMPOWERMENT RESET

Start practicing energetic awareness. Before making any decision, ask yourself:

- **Does this feel like expansion or contraction?**

- **Does this feel like love or fear?**

- **Does this feel aligned or misaligned?**

Your intuition always knows the answer before your mind does.

6. Stepping into Sovereignty: Becoming the Business Goddess

Building my business was never just about financial success. It was about stepping into sovereignty—the ability to create my own reality, free from fear, limitation, or dependency on external circumstances.

I no longer play small. I no longer ask for permission to shine. And the moment I claimed my power, I attracted clients, opportunities, and partnerships that resonated with my highest vision.

7. Embody the Energy of Who You Want to Become

Most people wait until they "feel ready" before they act. But the secret is this: you must embody the energy of who you want to become before the external world catches up.

SELF-EMPOWERMENT RESET

I didn't wait until I was successful to act like a powerful, confident woman. I stepped into that energy first, and success followed.

Start living as if you are already the person you aspire to be. Dress like her, speak like her, think like her. The universe responds to energy, and when you show up as her, the world will reflect that back to you.

8. Empowering Others to Rise

One of my deepest commitments is to help others break free from fear and step into their highest potential. I know what it feels like to be trapped in self-doubt, but I also know what it takes to break free.

We do not rise alone. Every empowered woman creates a ripple effect that empowers countless others. That is the essence of a true Business Goddess—not just succeeding for herself but lifting others as she rises.

9. Liberation Is a Choice—Make It Daily

Every day, you have a choice: to stay small or to expand, to let fear win or to claim your power. True liberation is not a one-time event; it is a daily decision.

SELF-EMPOWERMENT RESET

Ask yourself each morning:

- **How can I show up as my most powerful self today?**

- **What fear can I release right now?**

- **Who can I empower with my presence and my work?**

Power is a habit. Confidence is a practice. The more you choose liberation, the more natural it becomes.

Your Time is Now

I started this journey with nothing but faith, resilience, and a deep knowing that I was meant for more. Now, I stand as a woman who has transformed her reality and is committed to guiding others to do the same. Every year I transform thousands of people lives through my international retreats, talks, online events and coaching. Many healers came to me to learn how to liberate themselves and step into their own power. Many coaches learned from me how to create bigger impact and go from serving 1:1 to empowering crowds… many couples now have a fulfilling relationship and raising their children in a healthy environment… and it breaks my heart when I think that all of that would not happen if I would continue play small and would not follow my purpose…

SELF-EMPOWERMENT RESET

If you are reading this, know that you, too, are meant for something extraordinary. Your fears, struggles, and challenges are not here to stop you; they are here to shape you into the powerful force you were always destined to be.

Step into your sovereignty. Trust your intuition. Align with your purpose. And most importantly—choose liberation, every single day.

Your time is now.

~ With love, Olga

SELF-EMPOWERMENT RESET

~ Olga Geidane ~

Book a 30 min coffee call with me here: https://calendly.com/olgageidane/quickchat

The next VSAI event is here: https://vsainternational.org/events/

Click here to watch my speaker's showreel: https://youtu.be/H6A7yqWDTiQ

Olga Geidane

New Life Kick Start

Former Regional President of PSA Yorkshire | Task Force Chair of Education at VSAI | NED & Chair of Center for Sustainable Action | Author

~ Acknowledgements ~

I would like to take this time to thank every single one of the authors in this book who have taken the time to share their vulnerable experiences with the public to help others move forward with ease.

I would also like to thank God for guiding me to write and publish this book together with the women that have come together in this book to help Inspire empower and help other women succeed. No egos no jealousy and no Envy just some pure-hearted women wanting to add to the world with some positive reinforcement on how to be resilient. With gratitude and love in my heart I present to you the Business Goddesses.

THANK YOU!!!

LOVE + LIGHT

Rev.Dr. Marianne Padjan

~ About The Author ~
Rev. Dr. Marianne Padjan

Marianne Padjan Is an International Award-winning Author and Coach. Marianne has received many prestigious awards and excels in all she does. Marianne is also a real estate agent and a Managing Director at APLGO. Marianne is also the CEO at MPowered Voice Publishing. Marianne is a leader of many hats and has made her mark in all places she goes. Marianne holds monthly summits and speaking events regularly.

SELF-EMPOWERMENT RESET

To get in touch with Rev. Dr. Marianne Padjan please contact her below:

Marianne Padjan | Real Estate Agent eXp Realty Brokerage
marianne.padjan@exprealty.com

www.exprealty.ca

Marianne Padjan, EXP Realty | Facebook

SELF-EMPOWERMENT RESET

SELF-EMPOWERMENT RESET

SELF-EMPOWERMENT RESET